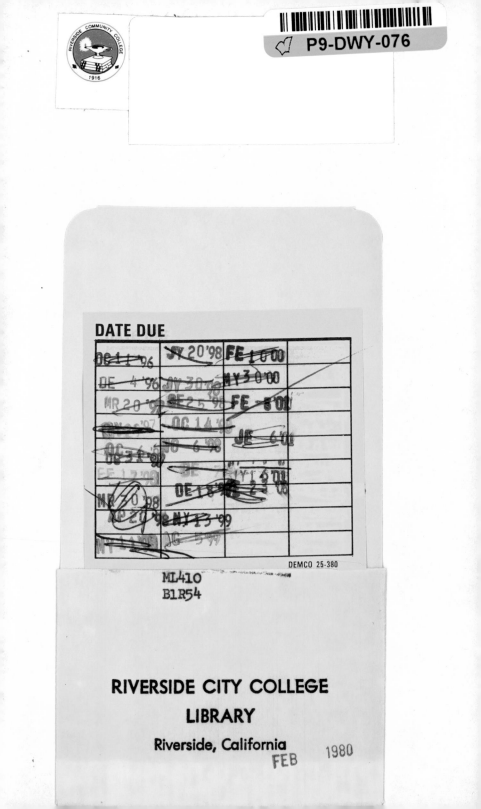

BACH

A biography, with a survey of
books, editions and recordings

THE CONCERTGOER'S COMPANIONS
SERIES EDITOR ALEC HYATT KING

BACH by Alec Robertson
BEETHOVEN by Rosemary Hughes
BRAHMS by Kathleen Dale
CHOPIN by Derek Melville
HANDEL by Charles Cudworth
HAYDN by Brian Redfern
MOZART by Alec Hyatt King

BACH

A biography, with a survey of
books, editions and recordings

by
Alec Robertson

CLIVE BINGLEY LINNET BOOKS
LONDON HAMDEN · CONN

FIRST PUBLISHED 1977 BY CLIVE BINGLEY LTD
16 PEMBRIDGE ROAD LONDON W11
SIMULTANEOUSLY PUBLISHED IN THE USA BY LINNET BOOKS
AN IMPRINT OF THE SHOE STRING PRESS INC
995 SHERMAN AVENUE HAMDEN CONNECTICUT 06514
SET IN 12 ON 13 POINT ALDINE ROMAN BY ALLSET
AND PRINTED AND BOUND IN THE UK BY
REDWOOD BURN LTD OF TROWBRIDGE AND ESHER
COPYRIGHT © CLIVE BINGLEY LTD 1977
ALL RIGHTS RESERVED
BINGLEY ISBN: 0-85157-230-8
LINNET ISBN: 0-208-01055-6

Library of Congress Cataloging in Publication Data

Robertson, Alec.
    Bach.

    (The Concertgoer's companions)
    Bibliography: p.
    "Editions of Bach's music": p.
    Discography: p.
    Includes index.
        1. Bach, Johann Sebastian, 1685-1750.
    2. Composers—Germany—Biography.
    ML410.B1R54   780',92'4 [B]   77-23211
    ISBN 0-208-01055-6

Contents

Bach's life   7

Books in English about Bach   53

Editions of Bach's music   72

Selected recordings of Bach's music   107

Index   130

I must thank Alec Hyatt King for bibliographical advice and assistance
with the preparation of the chapters on the books about Bach and the
editions of Bach's music; and Robert Anderson for his advice to me on
points of detail relating to Bach's life.

A R

Quotations in the text are from *Johann Sebastian Bach. A biography* by
C S Terry (Oxford University Press, 1928) and *The Bach reader. A life
of Johann Sebastian Bach in letters and documents*, edited by Hans T
David and Arthur Mendel (J M Dent & Sons, 1946).

Bach's life

On April 23 1843, a monument to the memory of Johann Sebastian Bach, erected largely owing to the advocacy of Mendelssohn, was unveiled at Leipzig.

It was a small act of atonement for the failure of the town's
civil and ecclesiastical authorities—and to a lesser extent its citizens— to recognize the true genius of the man who had been
Thomas Cantor (Cantor in St Thomas's church) for twenty-
seven years. Schumann noticed the occasion in his *Neue Zeitschrift für Musik* the following month, and concluded: 'Honour
was paid not only to Bach but also to his sole surviving grandson, a man of eighty-four, still full of energy, with snow-white
hair and expressive features. No one knew of his existence, not
even Mendelssohn, who had lived so long in Berlin and, he sup-
posed, had followed every trace of Bach he could discover. Yet
his grandson had resided there for over forty years. No information was obtained regarding his circumstances, except that
he had filled the office of Capellmeister to the consort of Friedrich Wilhelm III, and enjoys a pension which maintains him in
comfort.'

This modest old man, whose heart must have been filled with
joy at the tardy honour done to his grandfather, died on Christmas Day 1845, the last male Bach in direct line from the composer.

Bach took great pride in his ancestry, and in 1735 drew up
the first draft of the *Origin of the Bach family of musicians*, to
which additions were made by Carl Philipp Emanuel, his second

7

son, and by others. Bach's chief interest naturally lay in the musical members of his clan, and especially in those who were composers (he delighted also in performing their works). It seems eminently fitting that the achievements of all his forbears should be summed up and beyond all measure surpassed in this one supremely great flowering of the Bach tree. Bach's sons, Wilhelm Friedemann and, even more, Carl Philipp Emanuel, naturally followed the exciting trends of the new harmonic age. They loved and admired their great father but, like their contemporaries, considered his predominantly contrapuntal mode of expression a thing of the past.

It is perhaps a pity that the most often-reproduced portrait of Bach is the one painted in 1746 by Elias Gottlieb Haussmann and commissioned by the composer to be presented, as was required of all new members, to the Society of Musical Sciences. It has the stiffness of an official portrait, and the artist has carefully detailed the triple canon for six voices that Bach is holding as his offering to the society. His expression is severe and made more so because of the strained look in his eyes, occasioned by years of writing his own music and copying that of others. A more engaging personality looks out at us from the pastel portrait (c1733) by Gottlieb Friedrich Bach (1714-1785), organist and court painter at Meiningen, eldest son of the court composer and conductor Johann Ludwig Bach (1677-1731), whose church cantatas Bach frequently performed in Leipzig. A desire to see what Bach looked like in earlier years makes one inclined to accept a portrait now in the Erfurt Museum though not fully authenticated. It is labelled 'Johann Sebastian Bach, Concertmeister and Court Organist in Weimar', and may possibly be the work of the Weimar court painter, Johann Ernst Reutsch the elder. Bach is shown at about the age of thirty in court dress, with the expression of one listening attentively to a friend, and there is humour in the curve of the mouth.

Some of the few reported sayings of Bach have a delightfully shrewd touch of humour, as shown by the first entry in the *Origin of the Bach family of musicians*. It refers to Vitus Bach (d1619), founder of the clan and described as a miller in Hungary, who had to flee to Germany on account of his Lutheran religion. He eventually settled at Wechmar, near Gotha, in the province of Thuringia, and carried on his trade there. 'He found his greatest pleasure in a little cittern', Bach tells us, 'which he took with him even into the mill and played while the grinding was going on. (How pretty it must have sounded together! However, it taught him to keep time, and that apparently is how music first came into our family.)'

The *Origin* shows a succession of the Bachs working in the towns of Thuringia, mostly in Arnstadt, and after that, up to the birth of Sebastian, in Erfurt and Eisenach. Johannes (1604-73) is the first town musician and organist (at Erfurt), Georg Christoph (1642-97) the first cantor in the list (in Themar, and later in Franconia at Schweinfurt). The most interesting is Johann Christoph (1643-1703), court and town organist at Eisenach and a first cousin of Bach's father. Bach rated Johann Christoph as 'a profound composer', and C P E added, 'This is the great and expressive composer'. Under his own name Bach merely lists the various posts he held, stating that in 1723 he was called from Cöthen 'to become Music Director and Cantor at the *Thomas-Schule*, in Leipzig; where, in accordance with God's Holy Will, he still lives . . .'. C P E adds: 'He died (from a stroke at Leipzig), in 1750 on the 30th [in fact, the 28th] of July'.

The Bach family was close-knit. If one of them was in trouble, there was certain to be a member of the clan to come to the rescue. If one of them applied for a post, there might well be another able to pull strings to further his chances. If one left his children orphaned, they would be sheltered under the roof of another—as was Bach himself.

CHILDHOOD

Bach was born at Eisenach on March 21 1685 (a bare month after Handel was born at Halle, some thirty miles off) and was

9

christened Johann Sebastian, after his two godfathers. There were at least thirty Bachs with Johann for one of their names, but Bach was the first Sebastian. The only other Bach thus baptised was Carl Philipp Emanuel's second son. The younger J S B, however, had no mind to bear such a burden, and with Bach-like independence substituted Samuel for Sebastian in order to make it perfectly clear music was not for him. He turned to painting, for which he showed genuine talent, and died in Rome at the age of thirty.

St George's Church, Eisenach, in which Bach was baptised, was full of history. Here Luther had preached continuing defiance of Rome on May 3 1521, after his appearance before the Reichstag at Worms. And recently there has been a tradition, whenever a baby is christened at St George's, that the pastor should refer to the birth of Sebastian. His father, Johann Ambrosius Bach, had married Elisabeth Lämmerhirt, daughter of a councillor at Erfurt. There were eight children of the marriage. Ambrosius seems to have been a delightful character. A portrait of him, possibly by an official of the Eisenach court, and inherited by C P E, shows him in casual dress, without a wig and with shirt open at the neck. Geiringer describes the portrait thus: 'His attitude is not stiff and ceremonious, but easy and natural, so as to give the impression that he has just made music in his workroom, through the window of which the Eisenach Wartburg is to be seen. The strong throat, the massive chin, and the bold fleshy nose, features his son Sebastian was to inherit, seem to proclaim the stubborn tenacity of the Bach clan. His shrewd eyes and dark hair complete the picture of a full-blooded, vigorous and somewhat earthy personality.' (Ambrosius is said to have been a fine executant, skilled in singing and in the playing of violin and viola, though he was not a composer.)

We know little of Sebastian's early years. Perhaps we may suppose that his father taught him to play stringed instruments, and that on occasions he sat beside Johann Christoph, 'the profound composer', in the organ loft at St George's. This could have been a powerful influence in his young life. His great-grandfather, grandfather and father were engaged mainly in secular music, but the tradition of serving the church, equally strong among the Bachs, revived in Sebastian.

At the age of eight Sebastian entered the Eisenach Latin School, where the curriculum involved him in the biblical studies that interested him throughout his life. His first biographer, Johann Nicolaus Forkel, tells us on the evidence of C P E Bach that Sebastian had a fine and penetrating soprano voice of great range and flexibility, and that he quickly graduated from the choir which was capable of singing only hymns to the choir that performed cantatas and motets.

When he was nine, Sebastian's mother died and his father married again for the sake of his large family. But within twelve months he himself died, on February 20 1695. In trouble, as has been said, the Bachs rallied to one another, and now, to ease the widow's burden, Sebastian and his brother Jacob were taken into the house of their newly-married eldest brother Johann Christoph, the twenty-three year old organist at Ohrdruf, a little Thuringian town between Arnstadt and Eisenach. Johann was almost a stranger to his brothers, having left home some years before to study in Erfurt with the great organist Johann Pachelbel. His wife was expecting a child, and it was not easy for him to support two brothers as well on his small salary. In fact Jacob, after a year at Ohrdruf, returned to Eisenach as apprentice to his father's successor in the post of town musician. Jacob's further career, so different in the distances travelled from that of Sebastian, is given in the *Origin*: 'After a few years, namely Anno 1704, he entered the service of the Royal Swedish Army'. At this point Sebastian wrote a *Capriccio on the departure of his beloved brother* (992)', a programme piece for harpsichord with movement titles such as 'picturing of various calamities that might overtake him in foreign parts', 'general lamento of the friends', 'fugue in imitation of the postilion's horn'. With Charles XII he continued as far as Bender in Turkey. Philipp Emanuel noted in the *Origin* that from 'Bender he journeyed to Constantinople, and there had instruction on the flute from the famous flautist Buffardin . . . This

11

information was furnished by Buffardin himself when he once visited J S Bach in Leipzig.' Johann Jacob eventually died at Stockholm in 1722.

Sebastian, who was able as a singer to contribute to his keep, stayed on for five years, during which he profited from the high standard of the Ohrdruf school, where Luther himself had studied. Sebastian's academic record at Ohrdruf was distinguished, and shows him to have had a natural flair for other subjects besides music.

The celebrated incident of his procuring and copying a coveted manuscript volume of pieces by such notable musicians as Froberger, Pachelbel, Buxtehude and Böhm, denied to him by his brother, is perhaps not altogether credible. Forkel asks us to believe that he was able to extract it from a bookcase with latticed front, rolling it up for the purpose, copying it out painfully by moonlight as he was not allowed a candle in his bedroom, and then returning it and unrolling it when it was back on its shelf. His brother, on discovering what had happened, confiscated the volume; Sebastian recovered it only at his death 'soon after'. In reality, Johann Christoph lived till 1721, and that Sebastian bore him no ill will is shown by the fact that he dedicated to him a Capriccio (993), one of his earlier clavier pieces, perhaps even written by the time he left Ohrdruf (it is clearly prentice work).

The real importance of this story lies in the indication of Sebastian's avid curiosity about other men's music, a characteristic which lasted all his life, and in the ability it suggests he already possessed to look after his own musical education. The accommodation in Johann's house became strained with the arrival of his first two children, and it was time for Sebastian, now almost fifteen, to fend for himself.

APPRENTICESHIP

It was probably through Elias Herda, the new Cantor of the Ohrdruf school faculty, that Sebastian and an older school friend, Georg Erdmann, were able to set out on the 200-mile

12

journey to Lüneburg in northern Germany, assured of places in the *Mettenchor* (the boys' choir) of St Michael's church. Herda had held a scholarship there, and though the school was interested mainly in younger boys or those whose voices had broken (as Erdmann's had), his favourable report on Sebastian evidently persuaded the authorities to make an exception and grant young Bach a scholarship. According to the Ohrdruf records, he 'left for Lüneburg on account of insufficient school funds'.

The monks of St Michael, a Benedictine foundation, had been loyal to the unreformed faith till 1532. In 1656 the monastery became a Ritterakademie, one of the earliest schools for the sons of the nobility, started in the seventeenth century. Their education was directed to the civil and military obligations of their rank, and the curriculum did not include music. This, on Sundays and at festivals, was provided by the *Mettenchor*. The fifteen or so boys in it had to be, by statute, 'the offspring of poor people, with nothing to live on, but possessing good voices'. They were housed and taught free, given pocket money once a month, and entitled to a share of the choir's earnings. They were educated at St Michael's Latin school, and here Sebastian continued his studies in religion, Greek and Latin. But more important for the development of the young composer was the magnificent library of choral music assembled over the years by successive cantors at St Michael's. At the death of Praetorius in 1695 there were 1,102 titles in the catalogue.

French influence was powerful at the Ritterakademie. The students spoke French, performed French plays, and were instructed in dancing to French music by Thomas de la Selle (a former pupil of Lully). Perhaps it was he who took Sebastian on a visit to Celle, the seat of the Dukes of Brunswick-Lüneburg, where there was a permanent orchestra of sixteen players and la Selle was also employed. The reigning Duke had a French wife and saw his court as a miniature Versailles. It seems probable, from the copies Sebastian later made of keyboard suites by Nicolas de Grigny and Charles Dieupart, that he was early fascinated by the French idiom.

While at Lüneburg, Sebastian had the opportunity of observing the restoration of the St Michael's organ; but the most valuable of his experiences, for which actual evidence is lacking, may have been to hear and perhaps to meet the famous composer and organist of St John's church, Georg Böhm, who had links with the Bachs in Thuringia. Böhm's influence can be traced in Sebastian's early organ music, and Böhm had been taught by J A Reinken, then seventy-eight but still organist at St Catherine's, Hamburg. Bach walked the thirty miles from Lüneburg to hear Reinken at his splendid organ, and may also have visited the flourishing Hamburg opera, where Böhm had previously worked and Handel was to arrive in 1703.

Sebastian was ready to leave St Michael's by Easter 1702. Nothing is known of his achievements there, but he appears not to have become a prefect. Had he now gone by chance to the university at Halle, he would have found Handel there, strongly inclined to music but studying law, and it is fascinating to surmise how these outstanding and very different personalities might have got on. In spite of Bach's efforts later, the two never met.

THE FIRST PROFESSIONAL POST

Bach wanted his first professional post to be in one of the 'Bach' cities, and so he travelled the 200 miles back to Thuringia. Three organist jobs were vacant at the time, at Sangerhausen, Eisenach and Arnstadt. Bach would have secured the first, at the church of St James, had not the Duke of Sachsen-Weissenfels intervened on the ground that a lad of eighteen was too young. At Eisenach, the post vacant through the death in March 1703 of Johann Christoph Bach was filled by Johann Bernhard Bach (1676-1749), a better known and older member of the clan. It is uncertain whether Sebastian applied for the post.

At Arnstadt, the 'New Church' of St Boniface, open some twenty years, replaced one destroyed long ago by fire. The one-manual organ was approaching completion, but until it was ready and his application could be considered, Bach had to

14

keep himself. So he became 'lackey and violinist' to Johann Ernst, the musical younger brother of the Duke of Weimar, in whose establishment he may well have taken part in Italian concertos and chamber music (the Corelli op 5 violin sonatas had been published in 1700). He also played the organ on occasions as deputy to the court organist. By good luck, Martin Feldhaus, Mayor of Arnstadt, was a distant relative and, on the strength of the impression Bach's organ playing had made at the Weimar court, he persuaded the Council to engage Sebastian to test the new organ. The Arnstadt citizens were impressed by the young man's mastery, and no other candidates were considered.

Bach's work at the New Church started on August 14 1703. It left him plenty of free time, as he was required to play only three days a week. There was no cantor, and Bach's contract did not specify choir-training duties; it was assumed, though, that he would organise singers from among the boys at the local Latin school. Bach had been urged at his appointment 'to cultivate the fear of God, sobriety and the love of peace'; the third requirement sometimes eluded Bach in his dealings with the ill-assorted choir. He was at no time a good disciplinarian; and some of the singers were considerably older than he was. The student Geyersbach, whose person or bassoon Bach had insulted so grievously that a street fight ensued, was already twenty-one when Bach came to Arnstadt. He had little patience with his incompetent singers, the less so because it was not officially part of his duties to train and conduct them. He found consolation in the company of his second cousin, Maria Barbara, an orphan like himself, who lived in the house of the mayor. Here Bach boarded too for a time, and the young couple fell in love.

Arnstadt was an attractive enough place to live in, but Bach could never have been content with its artistic prospects. Ambitious for his own development, he turned his thoughts to Lübeck, over 200 miles distant, where the great organist and composer Dietrich Buxtehude lived and annually directed the famous *Abendmusiken* (evening concerts) at St Mary's. Bach applied for, and was granted, a month's leave of absence and left as substitute his cousin Johann Ernst. In the event, Bach stayed away not four weeks but four months, without a word to the Consistory.

At Lübeck he heard large musical forces for the first time. They consisted of up to forty instrumentalists, placed on four platforms, and the church's regular choir. When, at last, he tore himself away from Lübeck, he lingered on his way back at Hamburg to pay his respects to Reinken and, at Lüneburg, to Böhm, only reaching Arnstadt at the end of January 1706. No doubt word went round among the congregation of the New Church that their young organist had returned. But they were in for a shock! Bach's accompaniments to the hymns no longer simply led and supported their singing. His ornamentations, counter-melodies and strange harmonisations confused them, and they became impatient also with his wayward interpolations between the verses. Bach had not apologised for so grossly over-staying his leave, nor was he going to apologise for what he had learned from Buxtehude. Since he now seemed to take no notice of criticism, he was eventually summoned before the Consistory on February 21 1706.

The minutes of the meeting give the chief charges against him: 'Complaints have been made to the Consistory that you now accompany the hymns with surprising variations and irrelevant ornaments, which obliterate the melody and confuse the congregation . . . There is another matter: we are surprised that you have given up performing concerted music, and conclude that the omission is due to your bad relations with the pupils of the Latin school. We must therefore ask you to tell us explicitly that you are prepared to rehearse them in concerted music as well as in the hymns. We cannot provide a Cantor, and you must tell us categorically, yes or no, whether you will do what we require. If you will not, we must find an organist who will.'

Bach now knew he must comply or be replaced; and he was given a week to make up his mind. In fact Bach spent seven more obstinate months at Arnstadt without submitting to the conditions laid down. Rambach, the choir prefect, when reproved for a visit to the wine cellar during the sermon and for various disorders in the church, defended himself by attacking Bach and his way with the voluntaries: [He] had previously played rather too long, but after his attention had been called to it by the Superintendent, he had at once gone to the other extreme and made it too short'. On November 11 1706, the Consistory again summoned him before them, to be reproved for persistent neglect to rehearse the choir, and made it clear this time that, unless he did so, dismissal would follow. He was also asked to explain the presence in the organ gallery of a young girl, who had been heard singing to his accompaniment when he practised. Spitta suggests that this was his cousin Maria Barbara.

THE MOVE TO MUHLHAUSEN, AND MARRIAGE

For the moment Bach made no promises, but declared, as before, that he would give an answer to the Consistory after reflection. His remarkable abilities were becoming known outside Arnstadt, and it is possible that about this time he received an offer from the church of St Blaise, in the Free Imperial City of Mühlhausen, where the organist, Johann Georg Ahle, had died on December 2 1706. But as Bach did not have his test for the post until April 24 (Easter Day) 1707, it seems likely that, as later at Leipzig, other candidates had preceded him. Maria Barbara happened to be related to one of the Mühlhausen civic councillors, Johann Bellstedt. On May 27 it was decided at a parish meeting that consideration should 'first be given to the man named Pach [sic] from Arnstadt, who had recently done his trial playing at Easter'; Bellstedt was asked to negotiate with Bach for a further interview. On June 14 Bach stated his terms, requesting the same salary as he had received at Arnstadt (more than the experienced Ahle had been paid), plus the grain, wood and faggots that traditionally went with the job.

The church of St Blaise, 'dignified and comely under its twin spires' and beautiful within, must have delighted Bach, but the organ, a much larger one than he had had at Arnstadt, was in need of attention and repair. He took up his duties on, or shortly after, September 15 1707, but in October he returned to Arnstadt for his marriage to Maria Barbara. In August his uncle Tobias Lämmerhirt had died, leaving him a small legacy of fifty gulden; this greatly facilitated the setting up of his household at Mühlhausen. According to the Arnstadt marriage register, Mr Johann Sebastian Bach and 'Mistress Maria Barbara, youngest daughter and lawful issue of the late Master John Michael Bach, organist in Gehren, were united in marriage in Dornheim on October 17. The fees were remitted.' The pastor, Johann Lorenz Stauber, was a friend of Bach's and was later to marry Maria Barbara's aunt.

It is possible that Bach composed the funeral cantata *Gottes Zeit ist die allerbeste Zeit* ('God's time is the best', 106) in memory of his uncle; the music of this deeply felt work suggests personal involvement rather than an official occasion. Bach had not been long in his new post before he had to compose a large-scale cantata for the annual inauguration of the City Council, held in the splendid church of St Mary. This cantata, *Gott ist mein König* ('God is my King', 71) was performed on February 4 1708; it was directed by Bach and the church organist played continuo. The music shows what Bach had learnt from Buxtehude, particularly the division of the orchestra into four groups partly used antiphonally; and the fact that it was printed suggests that his employers had been duly impressed.

On February 21 1708, a parish meeting was informed that 'the new organist, Mr Bach, had observed various defects in the organ of the church of St Blaise and had submitted in writing a project for remedying them and perfecting the instrument'. Bach's meticulous specification already shows the knowledge which in later years caused builders some apprehension when he came to test an instrument, and started by drawing all the stops to test its lungs! His model seems to have been the organ at St George's, Eisenach, the restoration of which had been planned by Johann Christoph Bach (whose third son eventually succeeded Bach at Mühlhausen).

18

G C Eilmar, the pastor of St Mary's, belonged, as Bach did, to the orthodox party of the Lutheran Church; whereas J A Frohne, the pastor of St Blaise's, belonged to the Pietist party. A most unedifying warfare broke out between the two pulpits and congregations. As a friend of Eilmar's, Bach may possibly have been torn in his loyalties, though there is not the slightest evidence he became involved in the quarrel. Spiritually he had much in common with the very personal religion of the Pietists, but as a composer, he could not sympathise with their desire for only the simplest music in church. Before long an invitation to serve as a chamber musician in the *Capelle* (a body of musicians attached to a court, whose duties were mainly but not exclusively liturgical) of Wilhelm Ernst, Duke of Sachsen-Weimar, provided him with an opportunity for promotion.

On June 25 1708 Bach sent a courteous letter of resignation to his employers; it included only one reference to the conditions prevailing at St Blaise's: 'I have not been allowed to do my work without opposition, and there does not seem to be the least *apparance* that it will abate . . . Moreover, if I may say so respectfully, frugal as is my household, I have not enough to live on, having regard to my rental and needful *consumption*'. Earlier he shows, perhaps, some of the tactlessness that was to be so pronounced at Leipzig: 'It has been my constant aim to accord with your desire that church music should be so performed as to exalt God's glory and, as far as my humble ability has allowed, I have assisted that purpose also in the villages, where the taste for music is growing, and in whose churches its *performance not infrequently excels our own*' (author's italics). There was mutual regret at the parting, and Bach promised he would continue to interest himself in the rebuilding of the organ.

AT WEIMAR

When Bach's cousin moved in at St Blaise's, he did so at a reduced stipend—and by July 1708 Sebastian had settled himself in Weimar. At first he was both organist and chamber musician,

19

so that he was required to play violin in the Duke's orchestra and to dress up in Hungarian Haiduk uniform. There was no question of religious dissension at the court of Weimar, which Duke Wilhelm Ernst ruled with despotic authority. He was an orthodox Lutheran, no formalist but a man of deep and sincere piety, something of a scholar, separated from his wife, and without children. His brother Johann Ernst lived nearby and was co-ruler by the terms of an agreement originally made in 1629. There was little affection between the brothers, but Johann Ernst died in 1707, leaving a widow and two sons, the elder of whom, Ernst August, inherited his father's place as co-regent. This succession generated an even less harmonious relationship with the Duke. Bach had made friends with Ernst August and his very musical younger brother (who died in 1715) when he had briefly entered the service of their father in 1703. Both brothers had probably been his pupils, and he naturally resumed the friendly relationship with Ernst August. Later, however, this situation was a factor, as we shall see, in Bach's decision to leave Weimar for Cöthen. In the nine Weimar years Bach composed most of his finest organ works, though the instrument he had to play on was small and inferior to the one at Mühlhausen.

The Duke's life revolved round the baroque court chapel, where he first preached at the age of seven. The main feature was the baldacchino above the altar, which supported the pulpit and a lofty obelisk bedecked with cherubs. We are told that the Duke prescribed the order in which his courtiers should communicate at the Sunday *Abendmahl*, and was apt to question them about the sermon to see if they had been attentive. Lights were extinguished in the castle at 8pm in winter and an hour later in summer. When Bach took up his post, the plays and operas the Duke had previously promoted were no longer performed, but the Duke gave full support to concert music in the chapel. There was among his courtiers a distinguished man of letters, Salomo Franck, secretary to the Consistory, court librarian and numismatist, who had written two volumes of cantata texts. Bach set a number of these libretti after he became Concertmeister of the Capelle in 1714; he was clearly attracted by 'their mysticism, sincerity and feeling for nature'.

Meanwhile Bach's family began to grow. Maria Barbara was pregnant at the time of the move to Weimar, and her first child, Catharina Dorothea, was christened on December 28 1708. Two years later, on November 22, came Wilhelm Friedemann— 'that unstable son who most inherited his father's genius'; in 1713 twins were born and died on the same day, and on March 8 1714 Carl Philipp Emanuel was born.

In November 1713 Bach visited Halle to inspect a new organ under construction in the church of Our Lady. The pastor, well aware of his visitor's reputation, asked if he would be willing to undergo the usual 'test'. To this he agreed and forthwith prepared a *Stück* (*ie* 'piece', the name by which church cantatas were generally known). This cantata was probably *Ich hatte viel Bekümmernis* ('I had much distress', 21), which he designated 'for any occasion'. It was subsequently performed at Weimar and later revised for Leipzig. The text was almost certainly by Franck.

Greatly impressed by Bach's music and keen to secure his services, 'the Council of Eight' of the church of Our Lady sent to Weimar a lengthy document, styled a 'Vocation', offering 'the right worthy and learned' Bach the post of organist. One of the clauses required him to produce and perform an agreeable and harmonious cantata on high days and festivals and on the third Sunday in each month, in association with the Cantor and the town's musicians. Another clause stated that 'on Sundays . . . at Vespers and on Vigils he shall accompany quietly on four or five stops with the principal, so as not to distract the congregation, altering the registration for each verse, but eschewing the use of quintatons, reeds, syncopations, and suspensions, allowing the organ to support and harmonise with the congregation's singing, and stirring them with devotional desire to praise and thank Almighty God'. Bach does not seem to have taken exception to such rigid conditions, but the salary offered was less than at Weimar. As the authorities at Halle refused to make any alteration in the contract offered, Bach sent a formal letter of withdrawal, and was met with the accusation that he had only considered the offer to better his position at Weimar. The Duke, whom Bach had consulted, now promoted him to be *Concertmeister* at an increased salary.

In January 1716, Ernst August married the widowed Duchess Eleonore Wilhelmine of Sachsen-Merseburg, sister of Prince Leopold of Anhalt-Cöthen, who was to shape the next stage in Bach's career. A month or so after the festivities, Wilhelm Ernst attended the birthday celebrations of Duke Christian of Sachsen-Weissenfels, which included hunting and evening festivities in the castle hall. For this occasion Bach seems to have made use of his first secular cantata—*Was mir behagt* ('What me delights', 208), perhaps originally composed in 1713 and later repeated at Weissenfels and in Leipzig. This work, written to a classical libretto by Salomo Franck, contains an aria sung by the Roman pastoral deity Pales and known to us as 'Sheep may safely graze'.

For various reasons, Bach had become discontented at Weimar. On March 20 1715 his salary was again increased, and from the Weimar state archives we learn that 'the Concertmeister Bach is to receive the portion of a Capellmeister'. Nevertheless, when in December 1716 the Capellmeister Drese died, Bach was not chosen to succeed him. The situation was complicated by Bach's friendship with the Duke's nephew, Ernst August, since even the musicians of the *Capelle* were involved in the acrimonious bickerings between the two rulers. Prince Leopold of Cöthen, who had clearly been impressed with Bach's abilities, may have learned of all this from his sister, and was now anxious to secure Bach's services for his own court. The Prince was a talented and charming man, some nine years younger than Bach: he played the violin, viola da gamba and clavier, had a good voice and, as Bach said, 'loved and understood music'. He was also a Calvinist, and so Bach would not be called upon to compose much church music or be burdened with chapel duties, and his salary was again to be appreciably larger.

During the years at Weimar Bach had continued to learn a great deal about other men's music, and particularly that of

Italian composers. It was here that he arranged at least six
Vivaldi violin concertos for the clavier, as well as three for the
organ; here, too, that he copied out Frescobaldi's *Fiori musicali*—
Bach's manuscript runs to 104 pages. And it is just possible
that the opening chorus of *Weinen, Klagen* ('Weeping, mourning',
12), a cantata with Salomo Franck libretto, owes its chromatic
bass to a secular cantata of Vivaldi. Weimar was Bach's last official post as an organist, and he was succeeded by J M Schubart,
his earliest pupil, who had joined his household as early as Mühlhausen.

THE MOVE TO CÖTHEN

Conditions at Cöthen were attractive. The seventeen players
of the Prince's *Capelle* were provided with instruments of su-
perior quality; there was also a fine library of music which Bach
could draw on and study. The Prince's parents were of different religious persuasions, his mother a Lutheran and his father
a Calvinist. Leopold's father had given permission for a Lutheran church and school to be built in Cöthen, in spite of
strong objections from the Consistory. Religious squabbles per-
sisted under Leopold, but Bach was not involved. He and his
family could worship at the Lutheran church, and he could devote himself wholly to his musical activities, directing the *Capelle* and composing sonatas, orchestral suites and concertos in
astonishing profusion (much of Bach's Cöthen output has since
been lost).
    Early in 1719 Handel came to the continent in search of
singers for his Academy in England, and in the course of his
travels visited his elderly mother at Halle, only twenty miles
from Cöthen. Bach set out immediately—on one of the Prince's
horses—to meet his famous contemporary. But he was disappointed, for he arrived only to find that Handel had just left
for England. Here it may be added that ten years later Handel
was again in Halle, and on this occasion Bach, being unwell,
sent his eldest son Friedemann to Handel with the suggestion
that he might come to Leipzig; but he did not accept. Forkel

tells us how disappointed Leipzig music-lovers were that the two masters could not meet.

In January 1720, Bach, having perceived the great talent of his boy Wilhelm Friedemann, then nine and a half, seriously undertook his training and put together for him the *Clavier-büchlein vor Wilhelm Friedemann Bach*, which gives us such valuable insight into his method of teaching. It also includes, among other items, the compositions now famous as the two-part and three-part *Inventions* (772-801). Such a task must have given Bach much happiness, and he seems throughout his life to have derived pleasure from teaching gifted pupils. Forkel, on information from Philipp Emanuel, describes how Bach set about instructing young keyboard players. For six months to a year he liked to keep them on finger exercises: 'But if he found that anyone, after some months of practice, began to lose patience, he was so obliging as to write little connected pieces, in which those exercises were combined together. Of this kind are the six little *Preludes for beginners* (933-8), and still more the fifteen two-part *Inventions*. He wrote both down during the hours of teaching and, in doing so, attended only to the momentary want of the scholar. But he afterwards transformed them into beautiful, expressive little works of art.'

In Leipzig, Heinrich Nicholaus Gerber graduated from the *Inventions*, through a series of suites, to the *Wohltemperiertes Clavier*. Gerber's son recounts how Bach played Part I of the '48' 'altogether three times through for him with his unmatchable art, and my father counted these among his happiest hours, when Bach, under the pretext of not feeling in the mood to teach, sat himself at one of his fine instruments and thus turned these hours into minutes'. Carl Philipp Emanuel makes the point that his father was equally methodical in teaching composition. He would not take on a pupil unless he detected talent, and would turn away anyone he considered uninventive. But if accepted, his pupils 'had to begin their studies by learning pure four-part thorough bass. From this he went on to chorales; first he added the basses to them himself, then he taught them to devise the basses themselves . . . In teaching fugues, he began with two-part ones, and so on.'

24

In the spring of 1720 Bach sustained a cruel blow. In May Prince Leopold paid one of his visits to Carlsbad to drink the waters, and took his musicians with him. On returning in July, Bach was greeted with the news that his wife, whom he had left in good health, was dead and buried. We have no first-hand knowledge of Maria Barbara: she remains a voice that sang in the organ gallery of St Blaise's church at Mühlhausen, but shadowy though she is, the thirteen years of the marriage seem to have been truly happy. Bach's four surviving children were still young: Catharina Dorothea was barely twelve, Wilhelm Friedemann was ten, Carl Philipp Emanuel six, and Johann Gottfried five; and Bach had known himself what it was to be deprived at an early age of a mother's care.

Temporary distraction came in the autumn, when Bach was invited to compete for the post of organist at the church of St James in Hamburg, which, ultimately, he refused for reasons that are not entirely clear. Johann Mattheson gave an entertaining but highly circumstantial account of the affair in *Der musicalische Patriot*, 1728, six years after Bach had been appointed to Leipzig: 'I remember, and a whole large congregation will probably also remember, that a few years ago a certain great virtuoso, whose deserts have since brought him a handsome Cantorate, presented himself as candidate for the post of organist in a town of no small size, exhibited his playing on the most various and greatest organs, and aroused universal admiration for his ability; but there presented himself at the same time, among other unskilled journeymen, the son [Johann Joachim Heitmann] of a well-to-do artisan, who was better at preluding with his thalers than with his fingers, and he obtained the post, as may be easily conjectured, despite the fact that almost everyone was angry about it.'

In February 1721 occurred the death of Johann Christoph Bach, the brother who had received Sebastian as a child into his household. Meanwhile Bach had not given up composing, and in the spring despatched to Christian Ludwig, Margrave of Brandenburg, the six works now known as the 'Brandenburg Concertos' (1046-51). In the dedicatory letter, written in French, Bach reveals that the Margrave had commissioned the pieces

25

after hearing him play some two years before. Though he had certainly taken his time in completing them, Bach planned their despatch for his patron's birthday on May 14. He was also engrossed in work on the twenty-four preludes and fugues which were to comprise the first book of *Das Wohltemperierte Clavier* ('The well-tempered clavier', 846-869).

It was clearly essential for Bach to re-marry: he had waited a year and a half before deciding to do so, longer than was customary at this time. He chose Anna Magdalena Wilcken, daughter of a trumpeter at Weissenfels of Thuringian origin, and descended on both sides of her family from musicians. She was a singer in her own right, and was employed in this capacity by the Cöthen court. She retained her position after marriage, earning half as much as her husband, thus providing a useful contribution to the family finances. The ceremony took place on December 3 1721 in Bach's own lodging, by the Prince's permission.

Shortly afterwards, by a curious coincidence, Bach came into a legacy under the will of Anna Christina Lämmerhirt, wife of Tobiàs Lämmerhirt, the uncle from whose will Bach had benefited shortly before his first marriage. We know a good deal more about Anna Magdalena than about Maria Barbara. There are the two 'Notebooks', the *Clavierbüchlein vor Anna Magdalena* (1722), and the *Notenbuch* which he and she compiled together three years later, and which so touchingly reveals their loving relationship. Perhaps there are few things in the 1725 book more delightful than the poem, conceivably by Bach himself, with the title 'Edifying thoughts of a tobacco smoker'. Man and the pipe, it concludes, have many points in common, and its homely wisdom (almost worthy of Hans Sachs) conjures up an enchanting picture of Bach's Leipzig household. The fifth stanza alludes airily to matters the contemporary cantatas took very seriously:

How oft it happens when one's smoking:
The stopper's missing from its shelf,
And one goes with one's finger poking
Into the bowl and burns oneself.

If in the pipe such pain doth dwell,
How hot must be the pains of Hell.

Only a week after Bach's marriage, Prince Leopold—a very eligible bachelor up to now—celebrated his own marriage to his cousin Friederica Henrietta, daughter of Prince Carl Friedrich of Anhalt-Bernburg. The court celebrations lasted five weeks, and Bach contributed a congratulatory ode, which has since been lost. Leopold's bride was unfortunately quite unmusical and may have resented her husband's admiration and friendship for his Capellmeister. Bach later described her as an 'amusa', one quite uninterested in the arts, and the decline of the Prince's interest in his activities may have been one of the dominant factors in Bach's decision to quit his service. Another factor may have been the wish to give his older sons a university training such as Cöthen could not provide.

APPOINTMENT AS LEIPZIG CANTOR

The opportunity for release came with the death of Johann Kuhnau in June 1722, after he had served for twenty-one years as Thomas Cantor at Leipzig. Six weeks later, the town councillors responsible for the appointment to the Cantorship debated the merits of the six applicants, among whom Georg Philipp Telemann was the best known and the most favoured. This astute man declared that he was not prepared to undertake any extra-musical duties at St Thomas's school. This was conceded in view of his standing, and on August 13 he was officially notified of his election after undergoing the customary test. What Telemann really wanted was an increase in his stipend at Hamburg, and having played off one authority against the other and secured the increase, he withdrew from the Leipzig post. Bach had not applied because he was a friend of Telemann's, and after the latter's withdrawal, he still did not put his own name forward. But he was well aware of the difficulties the Council had in finding a satisfactory candidate. These now numbered five, including two Capellmeister, Christoph Graupner of Darmstadt and J S Bach of Cöthen. Graupner, an old pupil of St Thomas's school, was preferred but the Landgrave of Darmstadt refused to release him; he raised his salary as a compensation and made him other benefactions. When Graupner withdrew his application in May 1723, he warmly recommended Bach who had already, on Quinquagesima Sunday, February 7, performed as his test piece the cantata *Jesus nahm zu sich die Zwölfe* ('Jesus called to him the Twelve', 22).

As soon as Graupner's decision became known, Bach asked Prince Leopold for permission to leave his service, and the Prince granted it graciously and ungrudgingly. The Leipzig town councillors were by now fully aware of the exemptions that might be requested by an applicant. With a document addressed to them on April 19, Bach enclosed his certificate of discharge from Cöthen, and expressed his compliance with the conditions of service, except that he requested the 'worshipful council' to allow him, at his own expense, to delegate to another the duty of giving lessons in Latin. This was granted and the election took place three days later.

It cannot be said that the selection of Bach aroused enthusiasm. The attitude was rather, as one of the councillors said, 'if we cannot have the best we must make do with what there is'. Bach's fame as an organist was beside the point, as it was not a prime duty of the Leipzig cantor to play the instrument. But the stipulation made by one of the councillors that Bach's church music should not be 'too theatrical' could only be based on their reaction to the short trial cantata (22) already mentioned. (The *St John Passion*, 245, did not have its first performance on Good Friday 1723, as used to be thought, but in 1724.)

Before Bach left Cöthen Prince Leopold's wife died; but this did not alter his decision. The Prince would be sure to marry again, and did so two years later; this time he chose a music-loving wife, Charlotte Friederica of Nassau-Siegen, for whom Bach composed in 1726 a birthday cantata in which the Prince sang the bass part. The first child of the new marriage was born in 1726, and Bach dedicated to him his recently published first

28

Partita (825) for clavier. But in November 1728 the Prince died, and in the following March Bach visited Cöthen for the last time to perform in his memory a funeral cantata adapted mainly from the unperformed *St Matthew Passion* (244). So ended a warm, close friendship with a man Bach remembered the following year as 'a gracious Prince'.

The document laying down the conditions of Bach's appointment in Leipzig was signed by him on May 5 1723; it contained a clause that he was 'not to leave the town without the consent of the *Bürgermeister* of the year'. It need hardly be said that Bach flagrantly disregarded it and seemed also to forget the undertaking he gave at his installation on May 31 to 'show due respect to his superiors, and in general so conduct himself that his greatest devotion should always be observed'. Bach soon learnt that 'his superiors' meant the City Council, consisting of three burgomasters, the rector of the Thomas School, two deputy burgomasters, ten assessors who would keep a check on his activities, and the Consistory, the ecclesiastical authority responsible for the ordering of the services in the churches and chief arbiter in all matters concerning the music provided by the Cantor.

Faced with this forbidding assembly of high personages, Bach may have recalled difficulties experienced before in all his posts except Cöthen. But the possibility of sending his sons to a university as celebrated as that of Leipzig, the satisfaction of being able to influence the church music in so important a city, the need once more to compose regularly for the church (more than sixty cantatas date from his first Leipzig year) induced him to abide by a decision which was also to bring him much unhappiness.

THE ROUTINE OF THE THOMAS SCHOOL

The Thomas School in which Bach was to work had changed little since it was erected in 1554 on the site of an older building: it was outdated and overcrowded. The rector, J H Ernesti, was seventy-one and quite unable to exercise firm discipline over the foundation scholars, musical sons of mostly poor parents. The boys were overworked, badly fed and housed in insanitary conditions. One of the choir's tasks was to sing hymns at all but the meanest funerals whatever the weather; from this the boys and their teachers received small fees. Over a period from New Year's Day to the middle of January an ancient custom compelled them to sing daily in the streets to raise money for the foundation. The effect on their voices and health can be imagined. During Bach's first nine years at Leipzig six of the eight children born to Anna Magdalena died in infancy; out of the five born after the renovation of the school in 1732, only one.

The establishment at St Thomas had to provide singers for all four parts of the various choirs it furnished. During Bach's time as Cantor, most of the boys were aged thirteen to sixteen when they joined the school, and these were expected to stay a number of years; but others were admitted much older, four of them already having passed their twentieth birthday. And their musical attainments varied as much as their ages. (The following figures are all Bach's but they do not agree with the totals he gives.) Of the fifty-five foundationers, seventeen formed Bach's principal choir in 1730 and were capable of serving the chief churches of St Thomas and St Nicholas, at which elaborate music was expected; twenty could only sing simple motets at the two other churches, St Peter's and the New Church, needing further training, according to Bach, before they could be used in concerted music. The remaining seventeen Bach described as 'useless'. For his instrumentalists, Bach was able to draw on a body of professional musicians who played in the churches and fulfilled secular engagements. He describes them in 1730 as '4 town pipers, 3 professional fiddlers, and one apprentice. Modesty forbids me to speak at all truthfully of their qualities and musical knowledge.' And they could only provide two violins, two oboes, two trumpets and one bassoon (the apprentice). He could draw on the university for additional players, but they had been discouraged by the

30

council's unwillingness to pay expenses or a fee. For the rest, he had to depend on those of his singers who could play instruments, though only at the expense of weakening his vocal forces in the choruses.

Bach's routine was closely bound to that of the school. According to the regulations for the Thomas School published in November 1723, 'The bell rings at 5am in summer and 6am in winter, when every scholar rises, washes, brushes his hair, and is ready at the quarter-hour to attend prayers, bringing his Bible with him'. It was one of the duties of the Cantor to take his turn every four weeks as 'inspector' in the school. This involved saying morning and evening prayers, attending to disciplinary problems, supervising roll-call, and visiting the sick boys in the sanatorium. On Monday, Tuesday, Wednesday and Friday mornings Bach practised the upper classes in music. Thursday he had free, and on Friday he went with the boys to the 7am service. On Saturday he gave a lesson in Luther's Latin catechism, and in the afternoon rehearsed Sunday's cantata. The main Sunday service lasted from seven till noon, the cantata usually taking from twenty-five minutes to half-an-hour. Its text was often close to that of the Gospel and sometimes also the Epistle for the day, like the sermon that followed it.

Bach depended on fees for weddings and funerals to augment his income, but with a touch of humour he once remarked: 'Leipzig is such a healthy place that in this past year I have received from funerals more than 100 thalters less than the average'. In his free time Bach devoted himself to composition and, if his own works were not to be performed, to copying the works of others. His 'composer's room' was divided from the sixth form boys by only a plaster partition, so that he often had to work in noisy conditions.

FIRST QUARRELS

From the first Bach viewed himself at Leipzig primarily as a director of music rather than teacher and choirmaster, and to this end he usually signed himself 'Director Musices'. The implications of this attitude, perhaps natural to a man who had already been a *Capellmeister*, made for difficulties with the authorities. Before long, he came into conflict with them in various matters, including the selection of hymns to be sung at Vespers, this being by tradition the privilege of the Cantor. In early autumn 1728 the sub-deacon at St Nicholas made his own choice of hymns, and Bach refused to accept it. The Consistory upheld the minister's action and instructed Bach to accept the clergy's choice. On September 20 Bach protested in strong terms to the Civic Council, asking Their Magnificences to uphold the Cantor's traditional right. The Consistory, to whom his letter must have been sent, did eventually act against the use of undesirable hymns, not on theological but on practical grounds, as some exceeded thirty verses in length; the *Leipzig Song Book*, published in 1729, was to be the future basis for hymn selection in the town.

This matter was not finally settled till February 16 1730 and may have troubled Bach while at work on Picander's St Matthew Passion text for Good Friday, 1729. (Picander was the pen name of the Leipzig postal commissioner, C F Henrici.) He was certainly interrupted by the need, as detailed in the Cöthen court accounts, 'to attend to the funeral music for His Late Serene Highness, Prince Leopold, on the occasion of the interment, March 23 1729 and the funeral sermon, March 24 1729'. For this occasion Picander provided appropriate words to parts of the Passion already completed. Valuable time was thus lost when Bach should have been putting the finishing touches to his most ambitious Passion setting, first heard in St Thomas's on April 15. No account of its reception has come down to us.

For the two orchestras of the Passion Bach presumably made more use than usual of students from the university, and this was the year he took over the conductorship of the *Collegium musicum* founded by Telemann in 1705. He was now responsible for a series of weekly concerts held in Zimmermann's coffee house, and could thus make music in surroundings more relaxing than the practice rooms of the school. His work with the university men was always highly successful and bore out the advice offered six years previously by one of the councillors at his election to the cantorship: 'It was necessary to be sure to get a famous man, in order to inspire the university students'.

Bach's stupendous musicianship clearly won the respect of the young men over the years, and many of the students had lessons from him. How delightful this relationship could be is suggested by a testimonial Bach wrote in 1737 for Bernhard Dieterich Ludewig: '. . . he has not only acquitted himself well in his *studium theologicum*, but has also in various years frequented my *Collegium musicum* with diligence, untiringly participated in the same, playing various instruments as well as making himself heard many times *vocaliter*, and has in general so distinguished himself, that I have been impelled not only to entrust the younger members of my family to his conscientious instruction, but also to instruct him regularly myself in those things which he did not yet know in *musicis*'.

In May 1729 Bach was called on to fill nine foundation vacancies in the school. Twenty-three candidates applied, and Bach reported favourably on four of the trebles (including the thirteen-year old Johann Tobias Krebs, son of a former Weimar pupil), one alto, and two further names added at the end of his list (a soprano and tenor). He dismissed eleven boys out of hand as lacking all musical qualifications. The council responded to the report by admitting four youths rejected by Bach and another he had not even interviewed. When the Council met on August 2 1730, it was generally agreed that the Cantor 'had not conducted himself as he should . . . for which he must be reproached and admonished'. Councillor Steger spoke of the Cantor as one who 'does nothing, refuses to explain his conduct, and neglects his singing lessons, not to mention other instances of his unsatisfactoriness'. Syndicus Job described his as 'incorrigible'. By seven votes to four it was resolved to curb the Cantor's income.

Bach cannot have been unaware that there were grounds for these charges. He had by no means fulfilled all the conditions of his office. He was often invited away from Leipzig to give

33

his opinion on the state of an organ or to give an inaugural re-
cital; he usually failed to ask for leave of absence. He had not
found it easy to maintain discipline or to defer to his superiors
during the seven years he had so far held the Cantorship. No
doubt he gave too much work to Carl Friedrich Petzold, his
deputy for the Latin teaching, whom the Council found
thoroughly unsatisfactory. They rightly considered that 'the
third and fourth classes were the nursery for the whole school,
and accordingly a competent person must be placed in charge
of them'.

The deterioration in Bach's relations with the council was
temporarily halted by the death of Ernesti, the school Rector,
on October 16 1729, and the appointment the following June
of Johann Matthias Gesner, an admirer of Bach's from the days
when he had been Conrector at the Weimar Gymnasium. He
took steps at once to correct the lax discipline in St Thomas's
school and to have structural alterations made in the building.
Perhaps he could not fundamentally change the attitude of
Bach's employers to their stubborn and often tactless Cantor,
but during Gesner's term as Rector, Bach made no further protests to the council, and the council also seems to have left him
in peace.

Alfred Dürr's redating of many of the church cantatas (see
p 79) shows that Bach composed the majority between 1724
and 1729, and that the so-called later chorale cantatas date
from 1724 and 1725. This outburst of creative activity must
have strained him considerably: the charge that 'the Cantor
does nothing' was woefully wide of the mark.

In a document dated August 23 1730, Bach exposes some
of the reasons for the shortcomings in Leipzig music-making.
It is headed 'A short and much needed statement of the require-
ments of church music. With some general reflections on its
decline.' There is a sardonic note in the first words: 'To perform concerted music as it should be rendered, both singers and
instrumentalists are required'. Bach also made this interesting
comment: 'Now the present *status musices* is quite different
from what it was, its technique is so much more complex, and

the public *gusto* so changed, that old-fashioned music sounds strangely in our ears'. This from a man so often accused of being 'old-fashioned' in his own technique. He goes on to point out that German musicians are expected to play *ex tempore* any music put before them, whether it comes from Italy, France, England or Poland, 'just as if they were the virtuosi for whom it was written'. And this must be done, Bach complains, not on decent professional wages but by players who are under 'the necessity to earn their daily bread'. They had little time for practice, and Bach saw no hope of improvement till the council was ready to pay properly for its musical performances.

His document evoked no response from the council, and in his dissatisfaction Bach wrote to the old school friend with whom he had travelled to Lüneburg in 1700 and whom he had not seen since Weimar days. Georg Erdmann was now the Russian agent at Dantzig, and Bach dated his letter October 28 1730, giving him the news since they had last met and describing his disappointment, after high hopes, at the way matters had developed at St Thomas's: 'I am subjected to constant annoyance, jealousy and persecution. It is therefore in my mind, with God's assistance, to seek my *fortune* elsewhere'. He then asks if Erdmann can recommend him to 'a *convenable station* in your town'. He goes on to give a charming account of his family, in the course of which he proudly says: 'All my children are born *musici*; from my own *familie*, I assure you, I can arrange a concert *vocaliter* and *instrumentaliter*; my wife, in particular, has a very clear soprano, and my eldest daughter can give a good account of herself too'.

The fact that Bach, so tied to his ancestry and to Thuringia, so noted in musical tradition, in the faith and dogma·of the Lutheran church, should ever have contemplated the possibility of removing to Dantzig, is a clue to his disturbed state of mind.

The impulse passed, and with Gesner as Rector, Bach anticipated happier conditions in Leipzig. And so it proved. Gesner was friendly but firm with the students and did his best to soothe the ruffled feelings of the Council in relation to the Cantor.

Gesner, summoned at short notice from Ansbach, his birth-place, where he had been appointed Rector of the Gymnasium only the year before, came to Leipzig on September 8 1730. He was six years younger than Bach, an experienced teacher, a fine classical philologist, and a man of warm human sympathy. He had known Bach since 1715 and greatly admired his genius, though the delightful tribute he paid him in 1738 related—the all too familiar story—to his playing on the organ and clavier and to his conducting, rather than to his compositions. After he had left Leipzig for Göttingen, Gesner was working on a Latin commentary to Quintilian and introduced a playful comparison between the accomplishments of Bach and the ancient players of the lyre: 'He achieves what a number of your cithara players and six hundred performers on reed instruments could never achieve, not merely . . . singing and playing at the same time his own parts, but presiding over thirty or forty musicians all at once, controlling this one with a nod, another by a stamp of the foot, a third with a warning finger, keeping time and tune, giving a high note to one, a low to another, and notes in between to some'.

The enlargement and renovation of St Thomas's school set in motion by Gesner (two storeys were added to the building) made it necessary for the community to seek temporary quarters elsewhere. The Bach family probably went to the home of Dr Christoph Dendorf, situated near a brewery he owned.

In 1726 Bach had had engraved the first of the six clavier suites to which he later gave the title *Partitas*; in 1731 he issued the complete set, calling it *Clavierübung* . . . Opus 1 ('Keyboard exercise', 825-830), a title borrowed from Kuhnau, who had used it for two collections of seven suites composed in 1689 and 1692 (an advertisement of May 1730 suggests that Bach originally intended seven partitas himself, perhaps in imitation of Kuhnau). This same year Bach's son Carl Philipp Emanuel, now seventeen, produced his own Opus 1, a minuet for clavier, which he engraved himself. Forkel tells us that the *Partitas* won immediate success: 'This work made in its time a great noise in the musical world. Such excellent compositions for the clavier had not been seen and heard before. Anyone who had learnt to perform well some pieces out of them could make his fortune in the world and even in our times, a young artist might gain acknowledgment by doing so, they are so brilliant, well-sounding, expressive and always new.'

THE DRESDEN COURT AND BACH'S AMBITIONS

Augustus the Strong, Elector of Saxony and King of Poland, died on February 1 1733. His son Frederick Augustus II (1696-1762) succeeded him at once as Elector, but was not crowned King of Poland (as Augustus III) till January 17 1734. Like his father, he had become a Roman Catholic to ease his position in Poland, but he was in fact less interested in politics than the arts. Bach always had his eye on a court appointment, and though his object was not achieved till November 1736, he seized the opportunity provided by five months' public mourning (no Good Friday Passion or weekly cantata would be required in the Leipzig churches) to plan a work on the largest scale as an offering to the King. This was to be the Kyrie and Gloria of the B minor Mass, perhaps first performed on April 21 1733, when Frederick Augustus made a state visit to receive the allegiance of Leipzig.

There fell vacant in June 1733 the organist's post at the church of St Sophia in Dresden, where Bach himself had played two years before. This was the occasion recalled anonymously (the author was almost certainly A F C Kollmann) in an open letter of 1788, refuting Dr Burney's opinion that Handel was a better organ composer than Bach: 'Quantz, together with Hasse and Faustina—all of whom had known Handel for a long time and had often heard him play the clavier and the organ—was present in Dresden when J S Bach, in the thirties of this century, performed on the organ before the court and many . connoisseurs. They confirmed the opinion quoted, pronouncing him the first and most perfect of all organists and composers for this instrument.'

Bach now put forward as a candidate his son Wilhelm Friedemann, aged twenty-three. He played so brilliantly at his audition that he won the post. Bach was probably in Dresden for the occasion (he and Friedemann had visited the opera there together more than once), and he may have stayed on to deliver at the castle a letter which he had dated July 27 to accompany the parts of the B minor Mass, and in which he petitioned the Elector for a position at court: 'With profoundest devotion I offer your Royal Majesty the accompanying insignificant example of my skill in *musique*, with the most submissive demand that your Royal Highness may receive it not as its merits as a *composition* deserve, but with your Majesty's well-known clemency, and condescend to take me under your Majesty's most powerful *protection*. For some years past I have exercised the *directorium* of the music in the two principal churches in Leipzig, a situation in which I have been exposed to one or the other undeserved affront, and even the diminution of the *accidentia* due to me, annoyances not likely to recur should your Majesty deign to admit me to your Court Capelle and direct a *Praedicat* to be issued to that effect by the proper authority . . .'

There was no reply from Dresden, but Bach continued in his efforts to gain the title he desired. In August 1733 he produced a cantata (only the libretto survives) for Augustus's nameday. This may have been an adaptation of the work written to celebrate the reopening of the Thomas school in 1732. In September he composed *Hercules auf dem Scheidewege* ('Hercules at the crossroads', 213) for the birthday of the king's heir, and in December he honoured the Queen-Electress Maria Josepha with *Tönet ihr Pauken* ('Sound, ye drums', 214). Bach borrowed much of the music in the two latter works from the series of six cantatas, produced at the end of the following year and now known as the *Christmas oratorio*. The musical homage to the king continued into 1734 and included the performance of a 'Dramma per musica ovvero cantata gratulatoria'. The title page of the libretto explains the occasion: when the king 'together with His Most Serene Consort graced with Their Most

High Presences the Town of Leipzig at the Michaelmas Fair of 1734, the Students at the University in that place wished on October 5th, being the day on which His Majesty on the preceding year of 1733 had been chosen King in Poland and Grand Duke of Lithuania, to demonstrate their most submissive devotion in an Evening Serenade'. There were torches and illuminations; and Bach directed the *Collegium Musicum* in the cantata *Preise dein Glücke, gesegnetes Sachsen* ('Praise thy good fortune, blessed Saxony', 215), a score brilliant with trumpets and drums. One aria from the cantata was used in the *Christmas oratorio*, and the opening chorus became the *Osanna* in the final scheme of the B minor Mass. Bach received fifty thalers for this performance, of which about ten were due to the musicians.

On October 7 1736 another cantata, *Schleicht, spielende Welle* ('Glide, playful waves', 206) paid graceful tribute to four rivers running through the territories of the king and queen, and this was Bach's final act of homage before receiving his certificate as 'Compositeur to the Royal Court Capelle'. The document was 'done at Dresden, November 19 1736' and conferred the title on Bach 'at the latter's most humble entreaty and because of his ability'. The honour came at a time when Bach needed all the support he could get.

After only four years at Leipzig, Gesner gave up his rectorship in 1734 to become a professor at the new university of Göttingen. As evidence of Gesner's support for Bach may be cited two letters signed by both of them (and also the organist at St Nicholas) concerning a Leipzig merchant called Eitelwein, who had been married out of town. They were addressed to the council and the Consistory and made the point that 'In similar cases it has always been the rule that he who wishes to get married outside Leipzig is nevertheless obliged to pay the usual honorarium to the church officials and students'. The Consistory rewarded this display of solidarity by instructing the council to 'notify Eitelwein to pay the usual fees promptly, failing which he must be held to it by appropriate means'. Bach's feeling for Gesner is indicated by the fact that the

Rector's wife was godmother to Bach's shortlived son, Johann August (named, ironically enough, after the vice-principal Ernesti, one of the godfathers and soon to be Gesner's successor); and possibly it was for Gesner himself that Bach wrote a Canon, inscribed in January 1734 'as a memento for his good friend' and later numbered among Gesner's possessions.

BACH'S DISPUTE WITH ERNESTI

Gesner's successor was Johann August Ernesti, who had been on the staff of the Thomas school as vice-principal since 1731. He was still only twenty-seven when he became Rector, though an able and proven scholar. His ambition was to raise the academic standards at the Thomas school and devise a curriculum with less emphasis on theology and the classics and more concern with the newer disciplines. The musical tradition of the school, intimately linked with the religious life of the city, seemed to him something of a dead weight, made none the lighter by the extreme elaboration of the Cantor's now antiquated musical style, which was frankly unsuited to the material available among the boys at the school. But Ernesti's relations with Bach remained cordial enough at the outset to allow him to act as godfather to Johann Christian—the 'London' Bach who was later to hold the young Mozart on his knee—in September 1735.

In 1734 Carl Philipp Emanuel left home to continue his law studies at Frankfurt on the Oder, and the following year Bach was able to place his third son, Johann Gottfried Bernhard, as organist in St Mary's Church at Mühlhausen. In recommending the young man for the post, Bach could mention his own service to the town and could warmly praise his son's abilities: he 'has for some time past shown himself so *habil* in *Music* that I hold him fully competent to enter for the vacancy. I therefore, with all deference and submission, beg your Worship to accord him your influential *intercession* for the position he

aspires to, and to gratify my hopes by making my boy successful'. The application was successful, but at the beginning of
1737 Gottfried Bernhard was already auditioning at Sangerhausen, a place he eventually deserted because of the debts he
had incurred. Bach expressed his dismay to the Mr Klemm who
had furthered Gottfried Bernhard's appointment at Sangerhausen and in whose house he had in fact lodged: 'I must learn
again, with greatest consternation, that he once more borrowed
here and there, and did not change his way of living in the
slightest, but on the contrary has even absented himself and not
given me to date any inkling of his whereabouts'. Gottfried
Bernhard is next heard of at Jena University, where his object
was to study law and where he died in May 1739, four months
after his matriculation, at the age of twenty-four.

In the summer of 1736 began a dispute between Bach and
the Rector of the Thomas school that dragged on for the best
part of two years. The immediate cause of disagreement was
a young man, Gottfried Theodor Krause, of whose musicianship Bach thought well and whose scholarship was also admired
by Ernesti. He had been appointed prefect of the first choir.
The choral prefects, according to the regulations of 1723, were
four in number and 'appointed annually at Christmas by the
Cantor, with the Director's approval. They control the choirs
at funerals, and if the Cantor is absent act instead of him'.
Krause's attempts at discipline had led him to inflict corporal
punishment Ernesti considered unnecessarily severe. He in his
turn, by order of the Rector, was to be thrashed before the
whole school; but, being already twenty-two years old, he preferred to abscond. In his place as prefect Ernesti appointed
another Krause, Johann Gottlieb, who was not related to his
predecessor. Bach had auditioned him for the school in May
1729 and described his voice as weak and his musical proficiency
indifferent. Neither Cantor nor Rector had thought much of
his character at Christmas 1735, both agreeing that he was 'a
loose-living dog'; perhaps against their better judgment, they
decided to give him a chance as a junior prefect. But Bach's

main argument against the appointment was Ernesti's trespassing on the Cantor's responsibilities. On August 12 1736 Bach wrote to the council: 'The present Rector, Magister Johann August Ernesti, has, as a new departure, sought to effect the replacement of the Prefect of the First Choir without my previous knowledge and consent, and accordingly has recently appointed Krause, hitherto Prefect of the Second Choir, to be Prefect of the First Choir. He has refused to withdraw this appointment despite all the protests that I, in perfect good will, have made to him.'

It would be tedious to follow the dispute in detail. Between August 12 and 19 Bach wrote four lengthy letters of complaint to the council. He had turned the detested Krause out of the organ gallery; there had also been an undignified disturbance at Vespers. But Krause was incapable of distinguishing in his beat between three time and four time, so that Bach could not possibly let him conduct 'especially as the concerted pieces performed by the First Choir, which are mostly of my own composition, are incomparably harder and more intricate than those sung by the Second Choir'. Ernesti made a spirited defence, eventually suggesting that 'Bach's word was unreliable and his favour purchasable by bribery'. In February 1737 Bach took the matter to the Consistory, and in October he made his final move by approaching the King. In his appeal to the King Bach outlined the situation as he saw it and entreated His Royal Majesty 'in humblest submission most graciously to order:

(1) The council here to uphold me without injury in my *jus quaesitum* in respect to the appointment of the *praefecti chori musici* and to protect me in the exercise of that right, and

(2) The Consistory here to compel the Rector Ernesti to apologize for the abuse to which he has submitted me, and also, if Your Majesty please, to instruct Dr Deyling (Superintendent of the Consistory and Pastor at St Nicholas's) to exhort the whole student body that all the schoolboys are to

show me the customary respect and obedience that are due to me.'

A royal decree of December 17 1737 urged the Consistory to take the measures necessary to remove the grounds of complaint. We do not know what action followed, but the visit of Augustus and his wife to Leipzig in April 1738 may have provided an opportunity for healing the wounds. The occasion of the royal visit was 'the forthcoming marriage of Her Royal Highness the Princess Amalia to His Majesty the King of the Two Sicilies', when the university students presented 'a most humble *Drama* (since lost), which had been composed and was performed by the Capellmeister, Mr Joh Sebastian Bach'. Complete trust may never have been restored between Cantor and Rector but, at any rate, Bach was not again interfered with.

SCHEIBE'S ATTACK ON BACH

During the troubled year of 1737, Bach had to face an attack on his art from Johann Adolf Scheibe, son of a distinguished organ builder and himself no mean musician. In 1731 Bach had written him a testimonial, describing him as a 'most zealous student of music' and 'thoroughly at home not only on the clavier and violin but also in composition'. Scheibe had founded a magazine, *Der Critische Musicus*, and in its sixth number he made an onslaught on Bach the composer, though without mentioning him by name, giving unqualified praise only to his mastery of the clavier and organ. 'A musical composition', he wrote elsewhere, 'must naturally be pleasant and tickle the ear, it must also please the reason . . . Musicians must think naturally, reasonably and sublimely'. Hence Scheibe's view that 'This great man would be the wonder of the universe if his compositions displayed more agreeable qualities, were less turgid and sophisticated, more simple and natural in character. His music is exceedingly difficult to play, because the efficiency of his own limbs sets his standard; he expects singers and players to be as

43

agile with voice and instrument as he is with his fingers, which is impossible. Grace-notes and embellishments, such as a player instinctively supplies, he puts down in actual symbols, a habit which not only sacrifices the harmonic beauty of his music but also blurs its melodic line. All his parts, too, are equally melodic, so that one cannot distinguish the principal tune among them.'

One of Bach's friends, Johann Abraham Birnbaum, a rhetorician at the University, sprang rather lamely to his defence in a long-winded pamphlet of January 1738. When the controversy had degenerated to hardly more than an acrimonious discussion about the use of the word *Musikant*, Lorenz Christoph Mizler, a member of Bach's *Collegium Musicum* and founder of the Society of Musical Sciences, made the point that Bach could also compose in the modern manner when he wished to. Indeed Princess Amalia's *Drama* of the previous year had apparently been 'written in accordance with the latest taste, and was approved by everyone. So well does the Capellmeister know how to suit himself to his listeners.'

Scheibe was an accomplished journalist and therefore necessarily interested in the new ideas Bach had already ridiculed, probably as long ago as 1729, in the secular cantata *Der Streit zwischen Phoebus und Pan* ('The contest between Phoebus and Pan', 201). Pan represents the style of the dawning harmonic age, and Bach gives him an aria that shows how gracefully he himself understood it; but Midas is given a pair of ass's ears for his faulty judgment in support of Pan. Scheibe made some amends for his attack in a splendid review of the *Italian concerto* (971); writing in December 1739: 'It would take as great a master of music as Mr Bach, who has almost alone taken possession of the clavier, and with whom we can certainly defy foreign nations, to provide us with such a piece in this form of composition—a piece which deserves emulation by all our great composers and which will be imitated all in vain by foreigners'.

BACH IN THE FAMILY CIRCLE

In 1737, Johann Elias Bach, then thirty-three years old, came
to lodge at the Cantor's house while studying theology at the
university. His father was a nephew of Bach's father, and in
1743 Johann Elias became Cantor at Schweinfurth. He left
the household in 1742, having borrowed Bach's boots and rain-
coat for the journey; he then wrote to his 'most highly esteemed
cousin' a letter of thanks in which he expressed his appreciation
of the kindness he had received and his intention always to 'remember it with grateful feelings . . . I will not cease to pray the
Almighty daily in warm entreaty for the welfare of Your
Honour's whole highly cherished household, and particularly
to beg fervently for the lasting health of Your Honour'. Meanwhile he helped to draft letters for Bach and was responsible
for the education of Anna Magdalena's three sons. Elias's letters
suggest an attractive and warm-hearted personality. Early in
1739 he was writing to Cantor Koch of Ronneberg on the matter
of a subscription for the third part of the *Clavierübung*; later
in the same year he told Cantor Koch that Wilhelm Friedemann
had been over from Dresden for four weeks and there had been
'extra fine' music-making in the house; at the end of September
Bach was too busy to write himself, as he was rehearsing the
Collegium Musicum for the celebrations in connection with the
king's birthday.

In some of Elias's letters there are charming glimpses of Anna
Magdalena. He writes to Cantor Hiller, who lived at Glauchau
near Halle, to the effect that Bach had mentioned 'that Your
Honour possessed a linnet which, as a result of the skilful instruction of its master, made itself heard in particularly agreeable singing. Now since the honoured lady my cousin is a particular lover of such birds, I have felt I should inquire whether
Your Honour would be of a mind to relinquish this singing bird
to her for a reasonable sum.' On another occasion Elias describes
to Mr von Mayer of Halle the joy of Anna Magdalena at receiving six beautiful carnation plants: 'She values this unmerited

gift more highly than children do their Christmas presents, and tends them with such care as is usually given to children, lest a single one wither'. In the summer of 1741 Bach was visiting Philipp Emanuel in Berlin, and Johann Elias had to write to him about Anna Magdalena's ill health and the musical duties involved in the coming Council Election: 'Our most lovable Mamma has been very ailing for a week now, and we do not know whether perhaps as a result of the violent throbbing of her pulse a creeping fever or some evil consequence may arise; to which is added the fact that St Bartholomew's Day and the Council Election here will occur in a few weeks, and we should not know how we should conduct ourselves in respect to the same in Your Honour's absence. It is indeed painful to us to have to disturb Your Honour somewhat by such news in your present peace and contentment.' This very pleasant and affectionate relationship must have been a support to Bach and a solace to the often ailing Anna Magdalena.

SOME MASTERPIECES OF THE 1740s

In the last years of his life Bach produced much original work, but was also concerned with the completion and revision of earlier music. The most important project was the setting in order of the B minor Mass. To the Kyrie and Gloria of 1733 (and Sanctus perhaps from as far back as 1724) were now added the final movements of the Mass, a new and magnificently proportioned Credo, and other sections adapted from various sources.

Wholly original was the third part of the *Clavierübung*, written for the organ and designed as a musical illustration of Luther's catechism; Likewise the fourth part, 'consisting in an Aria with Divers Variations for the Harpsichord with 2 Manuals Composed for Music Lovers, to Refresh their Spirits', now known as the *Goldberg variations* (988) and published in 1742. They were commissioned by Baron von Kayserling, Russian Ambassador to the court in Dresden, who had known Bach for

46

about six years, at least from the time of Bach's royal appointment at Dresden, and had been present when Bach opened the new Silbermann organ in Dresden at the Church of Our Lady in December 1736. The variations were to be played by Kayserling's harpsichordist Goldberg, and the Baron handsomely rewarded the composer, according to Forkel, with the 'present of a golden goblet, filled with a hundred Louis d'ors'.

The second volume of the *Wohltemperiertes Clavier* (870-893) also dates from 1742. The title did not originate with Bach, but it seems probable that this further collection of twenty-four preludes and fugues was designed as teaching material for Anna Magdalena's children in the same way as the first part had been used for Maria Barbara's. In 1746 or later a former pupil of Bach's, Johann Georg Schübler, published 'Six chorale melodies of different kinds, to be played on an organ with two rows of keys and pedal' (645-650). Forkel describes these Schübler chorales as 'full of dignity and religious expression. In some of them we may see how Bach, in his choice of stops, departed from the usual manner. Thus, for instance, in the second chorale, *Wo soll ich fliehen hin?* he gives to the first keyboard 8-foot tone, to the second 16, and to the pedal 4, for the pedal has to perform the *cantus firmus.*' It so happens that the source of the one chorale mentioned by Forkel is uncertain; the rest are arrangements of cantata movements. In his choice Bach was clearly making a bid for popularity; at the same time he doubtless felt the music too good to be buried in cantatas that might rarely be performed again.

BERLIN AND THE MUSICAL OFFERING

In 1740 Carl Philipp Emanuel had been appointed accompanist at the court of Frederick the Great and, according to his own account, 'had the honour to accompany, alone at the harpsichord, the first solo that Frederick played as king'. Bach had visited Berlin in the summer of 1741 but had not been presented at court. In 1747 he again went north to see his son and was this time graciously received by Frederick. This may have been largely due to the kind offices of Baron von Kayserling, stationed in Berlin since he left Dresden in 1746.

The visit was reported in the *Spenersche Zeitung* of Berlin on May 11 1747: 'We hear from Potsdam that last Sunday (May 7) the famous Capellmeister from Leipzig, Mr Bach, arrived with the intention of hearing the excellent Royal music at that place. In the evening, at about the time that the regular chamber music in the Royal apartments usually begins, His Majesty was informed that Capellmeister Bach had arrived at Potsdam and was waiting in His Majesty's antechamber for His Majesty's most gracious permission to listen to the music. His August Self immediately gave orders that Bach be admitted, and went, at his entrance, to the so-called "forte and piano", condescending also to play, in person and without any preparation, a theme to be executed by Capellmeister Bach in a fugue. This was done so happily by the aforementioned Capellmeister that not only His Majesty was pleased to show his satisfaction thereat, but also all those present were seized with astonishment. Mr Bach had found the subject propounded to him so exceedingly beautiful that he intends to set it down on paper in a regular fugue and have it engraved on copper'.

Forkel also gives an account of the visit, derived from Wilhelm Friedemann, who had accompanied his father on the journey. In this version Bach's reception is more precipitate. The king was preparing for his evening concert and then, 'just as he was getting his flute ready and his musicians were assembled, an officer brought him the written list of the strangers who had arrived. With his flute in his hand, he ran over the list, but immediately turned to the assembled musicians and said: "Gentlemen, old Bach is come".' Forkel may have embroidered Friedemann's account here and there—perhaps Bach was not hurried into the king's presence without being given time to tidy up and put on his Cantor's gown—but Forkel's comment on the tale, 'I still think with pleasure on the manner in which he related it', is certainly disarming. During the tour of the Silbermann pianos Bach seems first to have improvised on the 'royal theme' a three-part fugue. Forkel continues: 'The King admired the learned manner in which his subject was thus executed extempore; and, probably to see how far such art could be carried, expressed a wish to hear also a fugue with six obbligato parts. But as not every subject is fit for such full harmony, Bach chose one himself and immediately executed it to the astonishment of all present.'

The next day it was the turn of 'all the organs in Potsdam' to experience Bach's improvisation. On returning to Leipzig, Bach determined to treat the 'royal theme' more fully. To the improvised three-part fugue (perhaps preserved substantially as Frederick heard it) he added one in six parts, and also a sonata in four movements for flute, violin and figured bass, plus two groups of five canons. Bach prefaced the work with a dedication recalling the happy circumstances of his visit and expressing his desire to make the 'royal theme' known to the world: 'In deepest humility I dedicate herewith to Your Majesty a musical offering, the noblest part of which derives from Your Majesty's Own August Hand'. *The musical offering* (1079) was engraved, not altogether satisfactorily, by Schübler, and 200 copies of the title page and dedication were printed by Breitkopf of Leipzig. A special copy was sent to Frederick the Great, but there is no record of any payment to Bach or gift in return. Nor do we know of any performance at the Prussian court.

Whatever Frederick may have thought of *The musical offering*, Bach was clearly satisfied with his work. In a letter to Johann Elias, now Cantor in his native town of Schweinfurth, Bach responds to his cousin's request for a copy: 'I cannot oblige you at present with the desired copy of the Prussian Fugue, the edition having been exhausted just today, since I had only 100 printed, most of which were distributed *gratis* to good friends. But between now and the New Year's Fair I shall have some more printed, and if then my honoured Cousin is still of a mind to have a copy, he need only give me notice upon occasion, sending me a thaler at the same time, and his wish shall be fulfilled.' In a postscript he speaks of Emanuel's two sons, the second of whom, 'about two weeks old', bore his grandfather's names.

Bach's request for the thaler postage from Johann Elias was as characteristic as his suggestion, in a letter of November 1748, that perhaps Elias should not send him any further casks of wine, as the customs dues were too stiff: 'My honoured Cousin can judge for himself that each quart costs me almost 5 groschen, which for a present is really too expensive'. In this same letter, the last we have from Bach, he announces 'the marriage of my daughter Liessgen (Lizzy) which will take place in the coming month of January, 1749, to the new organist in Naumburg, Mr Altnickol'. Johann Christoph Altnickol, organist, violinist, singer, composer, and a former pupil of Bach's, had been strongly recommended by him in 1748 for the Naumburg post as a man who 'understands perfectly how to treat an organ well, and take proper care of it, which qualities are inevitably required of a good organist'. Liessgen and Altnickol showed their affection by calling their first child Johann Sebastian.

Die Kunst der Fuge ('The art of fugue', 1080) was Bach's final extended project. Designed to illustrate the fugal possibilities of a single theme, this monument to Bach's contrapuntal skill was left incomplete. The scheme Bach would have followed in publishing the work is not altogether clear. The obituary compiled by Carl Philipp Emanuel with the help of two Bach pupils, Agricola and Mizler, suggests Bach's intentions: 'His last illness prevented him from completing his project of bringing the next-to-last fugue to completion and working out the last one, which was to contain four themes and to have been afterward inverted note for note in all four voices'. This evidence has been doubted, and it may be that the torso of the unfinished quadruple fugue represents all we have of Bach's intended finale.

By mid-1749 Bach's health had become a matter of some concern to the council, and he may already have suffered a first stroke. Count von Brühl, a minister at the Dresden court, had discussed the situation in Leipzig with the Vice-Chancellor

50

Dr Born and had strongly recommended Gottlob Harrer as candidate for the post of Thomas Cantor. Riemer's *Chronicle of Leipzig* reports the sequel: 'On June 8 by order of A Noble and Most Wise Council of this Town, most of whom were present, the trial performance for the future appointment as Cantor of St Thomas's, in case the Capellmeister and Cantor Mr Sebastian Bach should die, was given in the large musical concert room at the Three Swans on the Brühl by Mr Gottlob Harrer, *Capell-Director* to His Excellency the Privy Councilor and Premier Ministre Count von Brühl, with the greatest applause'. This tactless move—to say the least—must have been known to Bach, but Harrer had to wait for more than a year for his appointment.

Probably in March and April of 1750 two operations were performed on Bach's eyes by the Chevalier John Taylor, an 'English ophthalmiater'. They were unsuccessful, but during the last weeks of his life he may have worked on some of his uncompleted musical schemes and seems to have dictated an arrangement of *Wenn wir in höchsten Nöten sein* ('When we are in deepest need', 668), to which was added the superscription 'Before thy throne, my God, I stand'. On July 18 Bach's sight returned to him for a brief time; but he had another stroke and died on the tenth day, July 28.

In Berlin the *Spenersche Zeitung* made suitable mention of Bach's death 'from the unhappy consequences of the very unsuccessful eye operation by a well-known English oculist. The loss of this uncommonly able man is uncommonly mourned by all true connoisseurs of music.' In Leipzig Burgomaster Stieglitz spoke about the future at St Thomas's: 'The School needed a Cantor and not a Capellmeister, although he must understand music'. Carl Philipp Emanuel was among the candidates for the post, but Harrer was installed on September 29.

Bach left no will—strange for so methodical a man—and his estate was divided between his widow and the nine surviving children. Anna Magdalena was now in poor circumstances, and only Carl Philipp Emanuel appears to have taken a practical step to assist her by supervising the education of Johann

Christian. Anna Magdalena received some charity from the civic council, became an almshouse woman, and died in February 1760.

Forty years later an appeal was published in a Leipzig musical journal for Regine Susanna, Bach's youngest child, born in 1742; its terms were both startling and inaccurate: 'The family of Bach is extinct but for a single daughter of the great Sebastian. And that daughter, now no longer young, is— starving! '. The response was considerable, and Beethoven was moved to suggest the publication of a work of his on subscription to further the cause. Regine Susanna died in 1809, seven years after Forkel had published his biography of Bach 'as the first classic that ever was, or perhaps ever will be', and a few months after the birth of Felix Mendelssohn, who was to give so powerful an impetus to the Bach revival with his centenary performance of the *St Matthew Passion* in 1829.

Books in English about Bach

SOURCES

Although books about Bach appeared in English from the early
nineteenth century onwards, it was not until recently that all
the primary sources for his life were brought together in a single
volume. This is *The Bach reader. A life of Johann Sebastian
Bach in letters and documents*, edited by Hans T David and
Arthur Mendel (Norton, NY, 1945; Dent, 1946). It is indispensable to the English non-specialist reader alone 'for the collection
of the most significant material' it gives on Bach. The revision
of this book (Norton, NY, 1966) summarises in a supplement
the findings of research on Bach during the two intervening dec-
ades. But for details about the most important addition to our
knowledge of the composition of the church music, the reader
will have to consult Alfred Dürr's 'Chronology of the vocal
works of J S Bach in the *Bach Jahrbuch* (1957) which is discussed on p79.

The section of *The Bach reader* are: 1 Johann Sebastian
Bach: a portrait in outline (background, career and personality,
heritage and achievement, attitude toward the art of music);
2 Bach's life in his own writings and other evidence (this section
begins with Bach's birth in 1685, reproduces a large number of
documents of all kinds, from the entry of his baptism at Eisenach on March 23 1685, down to 'the specification of the estate left by the late Mr Johann Sebastian Bach'); 3 genealogy

of the Bach family by J S Bach (1735), with later additions
by C P E Bach and others; 4 obituary of Bach by C P E Bach
and J F Agricola (1754); 5 Bach as seen by his contemporaries;
6 'On Johann Sebastian Bach's life, genius and works', by J N
Forkel (1802); 7 the rediscovery of Bach—the story of his
fame from eclipse to the close of the 19th century (Mendelssohn's revival of the *St Matthew Passion* as recalled by Eduard
Devrient (1869); appendix—Bach on thorough-bass realization,
solutions of Bach's canons, bibliographical notes. The book
is illustrated with portraits of Bach and of his three eldest sons,
with topographical views, pictures of performances and instruments, and facsimiles of manuscripts and early editions.

Another important source-book is the *Catalog of the Emilie
and Karl Riemenschneider Bach Library*, edited by Sylvia W
Kenney (Columbia University Press, NY, 1960). This remarkable collection of editions of Bach's music and of Bach literature is housed in Baldwin-Wallace College, Berea, Ohio, and
runs to over 2,500 items. Though the entries in the catalogue
are necessarily brief, their presentation is exemplary.

BIOGRAPHY

In 1802 J N Forkel (1749-1818) published the essay mentioned
above—for it is that rather than a true biography. He drew on
the obituary of 1754 (*The Bach reader*, section 4) and on what
he had learned from his friends C P E and W F Bach. His sub-
title was 'for patriotic admirers of true musical art'. Forkel,
the son of a shoemaker, served as organist, music director and
professor at Göttingen university, and was the first German to
follow the example of Burney and Hawkins in attempting a
general history of music. His life of Bach first appeared in
English in 1820, translated by 'Mr Stephenson', a banker, of
Queen Square; and, a hundred years later, a new translation
came out, with notes and appendixes, by C S Terry (OUP; pb
Johnson, NY, 1970). Forkel presents Bach as 'the first classic
that ever was, or perhaps ever will be', and continued 'this man,

the greatest musical poet and the greatest musical orator that ever existed, and probably ever will exist, was a German. Let his country be proud of him; let it be proud, but, at the same time, worthy of him.' This resounding panegyric is based almost wholly on knowledge of the few engraved instrumental works, and some other, unpublished, vocal works, of which he possessed copies. Forkel also mentions five complete sets of church music (cantatas) 'for all the Sundays and Holidays of the year, five compositions of the Passions, many Oratorios, Masses, Magnificats'. He tells us that the annual sets of the cantatas were divided, after Bach's death, between the elder sons, the largest part going to Wilhelm Friedemann. But because of his financial difficulties, the latter had to sell his portion. Rather strangely, Forkel makes no comment on the worth of the vocal works, and has little to say about Bach's character or religion. But he does convey some idea of the sublimity of the organ works, and appreciated Bach's originality both in melody and harmony. Forkel clearly proclaimed that he was a great composer as well as a great performer.

Philipp Spitta's *Johann Sebastian Bach. His work and influence on the music of Germany, 1685-1750* was first published in German in two portly volumes (1873, 1880). The English translation, by Clara Bell and J A Fuller-Maitland (3 vol, Novello, 1884, 85; second ed 1899; reissued unchanged 1951, NY, Dover, pb 1962), is excellent, but the index, as in the German original, is deplorable. The book became, and has remained, the foundation of all modern Bach research and criticism, though later scholarship has invalidated some of Spitta's conclusions. He was the first of Bach's biographers to bring together all the available letters and other documents, to establish the value of watermark examination, and to print Bach's *Elementary instruction in figured bass* which includes the famous definition and comment '. . . the sole end and aim of general-bass, like that of all music, should be nothing else than God's glory and pleasant recreations. Where this object is not kept in view there can be no true music, but an infernal scraping and bawling.'

Spitta, of course, saw Bach through the eyes of his time, and though his constant theme is to present him as a classic composer, the result—when he comes to analyse his music—is distinctly romantic, as indeed he came to realise. He emphasises the poetic aspect in the organ chorales, but considered that 'the free vocal pieces in the cantatas, passions, oratorios, and masses lean far toward the domain of pure music, and seek to float the works on the musical stream'. But his rhapsodic descriptions of Bach's church cantatas, as compared with those of his predecessors, may be weighed against his theory of 'pure' music. Spitta's analogies are often very apt. In writing, for example, about the performance by his choir of the arias in the cantatas, he says, 'In Bach's own time an aria of his composition was, as it were, a lake frozen over: the boy's voice glided over the surface, careless as to the depths that lay below'. We can surely forgive such over-poetic descriptions of Bach's music—and the effect they had on later commentaries on his work—for much that he reveals is true and lasting. One of the most valuable features of his biography is the attention he pays to Bach's older contemporaries. He devotes for example some fifty pages to a most informative evaluation of Dietrich Buxtehude's works.

The first significant book in English not translated from a German source naturally leaned heavily on Spitta. This was *Johann Sebastian Bach* by Reginald Lane Poole (Sampson Low, 1882), which, though brief, is scholarly and perceptive. There is a useful general work, *J S Bach* by André Pirro, published in French in 1906, and translated by Mervyn Savill (Calder, 1957). It includes a bibliography largely of works on Bach in English and a discography of LP recordings, many of which have inevitably since been deleted. Pirro devotes 68 of these 196 pages to a good summary biography, which is followed by an illuminating study of the music. Some of his views were in advance of their time, and are still relevant. 'To be able to play Bach', Pirro wrote, 'according to Bach, one must learn to know him in his cantata scores. Any method of interpretation which is not based on a study of his works for choir and orchestra is merely a fantastic and deceptive method.'

The two-volume German edition of Albert Schweitzer's *J S Bach* (1908) was a greatly expanded version of *Jean Sébastien Bach. Le musicien-poéte*, published in 1905 at the time when he resigned as principal of the theological college at Strasburg and was about to begin his studies in the medical school of the university in preparation for work as a doctor in French Equatorial Africa. There was an immediate demand for a German translation, but Schweitzer found it impossible to convert his thoughts into German. He therefore wrote what was virtually a new book in German, twice as long as the French one, and it was the German work which Ernest Newman translated into English, with the text largely altered and expanded at Schweitzer's request. It was published as *J S Bach*, with a preface by C M Widor (2 vol, Breitkopf, Leipzig, 1911; A & C Black 1923; pb, NY, Dover, c1965).

The first volume includes a detailed account of the origins of the chorale texts and melodies and their place in the church service; describes the chorale preludes, cantatas and passions before Bach; traces his progress from Eisenach to Leipzig; describes his appearance and character, his musical journeys, his critics and friends. It also gives some account of Bach as artist and teacher, his death and 'resurrection', and is rounded off with a study of the keyboard, chamber and orchestral works and their performance.

This volume gives hints of what was to come—Bach's reflection of the text in his chorale preludes compared with the methods of his predecessors; the existence in *The well-tempered clavier* of a 'secret language of tone'; and the idea that the *Orgelbüchlein* is 'the lexicon of Bach's musical speech'. In volume 2 Schweitzer develops these ideas in chapters headed 'Word and tone in Bach', and 'The musical language of the chorales' and 'The musical language of the cantatas'. He declared that 'almost all the characteristic expressions that impress us by their regular recurrence in the cantatas and the passions resolve themselves into about twenty to twenty-five root-themes, mostly pictorial in origin', but says he will make no attempt to give a schematic catalogue of them. This, however, is exactly what he tries to do in the chapter about the musical language of the chorales.

57

It was the exposition of such ideas as these that caused Bach scholars to label Schweitzer's book as 'dangerous', while allowing that it contained much of great value. By many of us it will always be loved and read with gratitude.

Rutland Boughton wrote two books on Bach. The first, *Bach* (John Lane, 'The music of the masters' series) appeared in 1907. The second *John Sebastian Bach* (Kegan Paul, Curwen, 'Masters of music' series) came out in 1930. In the intervening years Boughton had become a political figure dedicated to Marxism, who proclaimed Bach as the champion of the peasantry. The 1907 book runs on conventional lines compared to that of 1930. There is no biography. The first chapter 'Bach and his time' is designed to show that Bach was not the 'great dividing line between the music which was scientific and dry and the music which is beautiful and human', and so due tribute is paid to his predecessors. In the chapter on the organ works, Boughton considers that the organ is the masterkey to a just understanding of Bach's style, despite its inability to render polyphony clearly. There is plenty to argue about in this small book: it shows a lack of historical perspective and illustrates the dangers of comparing the past with the future.

When Boughton wrote his second book he had, of course, become acquainted with the biographies by Schweitzer and Terry, and felt there was more to be said of the relation between the man and his work. He plunges straight into these dangerous waters in his first chapter. 'There was in the life of J S Bach a tragedy which has never been explored . . . Spitta seems to have been puzzled by it, Schweitzer alludes to it almost in a tone of annoyance . . . Terry referes to it sympathetically . . . The tragedy is that of an artist whose inmost nature and external material conditions are in irreconcilable opposition —who is forced by circumstances to devote his life to a kind of spiritual service in which he has no faith, and is necessarily false either to that service of himself'. That is the thesis worked out in this provocative, irritating, perverse but fascinating book.

It is over sixty years since there first appeared C Hubert Parry's *Johann Sebastian Bach. The story of the development of a great personality* (Putnam, 1909, revised by Emily Dymond, 1934). It is the product of a distinguished and penetrating mind, still very readable, though outdated in some respects. Parry naturally leant heavily on Spitta, and saw that Bach could not resist 'the device of realistic suggestion' in his texts, and attributed it in part to the 'extreme vivacity of his mind'. He emphasises that Bach's music 'is almost invariably intensely human in its expression', and, notwithstanding the enormous amount of choral music which he wrote, unecclesiastical. He bases his book on the development of Bach's 'unique artistic character'.

Bach. A biography, by Charles Sanford Terry (OUP, 1928; revised edition, 1932) is precisely what the subtitle declares—a biography, not a critical appreciation of the music mingled with biographical detail. Based on much original research, it is the only one of its kind in English, and arguably the best in any language. The revised edition contains so much more information than that of 1928 that the reader seeking the book from his public library should not be satisfied with the first edition. From start to finish, the work is eloquent of the author's love for Bach, and this, to many who confess to sharing it, makes of absorbing interest even the most trivial details used to build up the composer's portrait. The book is rounded off by seventy-four illustrations, well chosen portraits of the Bach family and pictures of their environment.

From his great store of Bach scholarship, Terry prepared some lectures which he delivered in America. They were published under the title *Bach. The historical approach* (OUP, 1930); the first lecture attempts to set the composer in full perspective and there is a long account of 'The Leipzig Cantorate in Bach's time'.

Terry made another invaluable contribution to Bach biography. *The Origin of the Bach family of musicians, edited with pedigree tables. A facsimile of Bach's manuscript* (OUP, 1929) is his edition of the famous genealogical notes made by Johann Sebastian and supplemented by his son C P E Bach. Terry appropriately received the dedication of Esther Meynell's *Bach*

(Duckworth, 1834, 'Great lives'), a small book written with affection and imagination in a charming style. Though some facts need correction in the light of later knowledge, it may be recommended to a public that does not feel able to tackle Terry's much larger biography.

Two important books by the American scholar Karl Geiringer may conveniently be considered together, both written in collaboration with his wife, Irene Geiringer. *The Bach family. Seven generations of creative genius* (Allen & Unwin, 1954) devotes nearly a third of its 486 pages to a succinct yet comprehensive study of Johann Sebastian, setting his life and music in the full perspective of his unparalleled musical ancestry and progeny. There is an excellent account of the works of his four musical sons. In the second book, *Johann Sebastian Bach. The culmination of a great era* (NY, OUP, 1966; Allen & Unwin, 1967), Geiringer views Bach not as a pioneer but as a summit, and to this end divides his creativity into seven phases. He shows clearly (to quote from a review of the book in the *Times literary supplement* of September 21 1967) how 'Bach's originality and sheer technical genius transformed his inheritance and planted in it the seeds of the revival that was to follow the half century of neglect after his death'. Some three quarters of the book is devoted to the music. A fascinating by-product of Geiringer's scholarship is his lecture on a controversial topic *Symbolism in the music of Bach* (Library of Congress, Washington, 1956).

Percy Young's *The Bachs, 1500-1850* (Dent, 1970), covers rather similar ground to Geiringer's *The Bach family*, but says rather less about the music. Despite lack of discrimination and some inaccuracies, it provides a useful survey. Similar ground to Young's book is covered by Celia Bizony's monograph *The family of Bach* (Artemis Press, Horsham, 1975), in which she describes its amazing development, against the social, religious and cultural background, with an illuminating account of musical patronage in the 17th and 18th centuries. The most recent general biography is by Jan Chiapusso, *Bach's world* (Indiana UP, 1970.) Though it is not entirely accurate, it does describe fully the intellectual climate of Bach's time and the far-reaching changes that took place during his life. Werner Neumann's *Bach. A pictorial biography*, translated by Stefan de Haan (Thames & Hudson, 1961), is a good example of its kind, with well-chosen, evocative pictures, and a readable text. It brings Bach's times to life.

Imogen Holst's *Bach* (Faber, 1965, 'The great composers' series), though primarily intended for young people, is so perceptive and well-written that it can be warmly recommended as a general introduction for other readers. It blends well-chosen illustrations with a good biographical summary, including some well-known choral and orchestral works reduced for playing on the piano.

This section may be concluded by mention of several books which touch on comparative history rather than specific biography. Friedrich Blume's *Two centuries of Bach. An account of changing tastes* (OUP, 1950, translated by Stanley Godman) offers a fascinating study of shifting values, from the time of Scheibe's attack on Bach in 1737, right down to 1941. Blume discusses Bach's influence on Haydn, Mozart and Beethoven and shows how little they really understood him.

One important stage in the rediscovery of Bach came in the early nineteenth century through the advocacy of several London musicians. Part of their revelation is recalled in *Letters of Samuel Wesley to Mr Jacob relating to the introduction into this country of the works of J S Bach*, edited by Eliza Wesley (1875; reprinted by Hinrichsen, 1958). These delightful warmhearted letters between the composer Wesley and an organist friend cover the period from September 1808 to February 1816; Wesley relates how he came to convince the hesitant and aged Dr Charles Burney of Bach's genius.

Because Bach and Handel were born in the same year and died in the same decade, they inevitably invite comparison. One admirably balanced account of their character and achievement is to be found in chapter 5 of R A Streatfeild's *Modern music and musicians* (Methuen, 1906). Archibald T Davison goes rather more deeply into the matter, in his *Bach and Handel.*

The consummation of the Baroque in music (Harvard University Press, 1951). He presents Handel as the popular avant-garde composer of his day, Bach as an obscure and conservative artist, and analyses their respective use of established musical forms in radically novel ways.

Another specialised, comparative study is Werner Menke's *History of the trumpet of Bach and Handel* (William Reeves, 1934), translated by Gerald Abraham.

GENERAL CRITICISM

The best general introduction is C S Terry's *The music of Bach* (OUP, 1933; pb Dover 1963), which he wrote as a companion to his biography. He describes it as a plain, non-technical guide, intended to relate Bach's music to the circumstances of his life, to unfold its extent, offer guidance for a more intensive study of it, and incidentally engender the 'warmth of heart of true enthusiasm' (a quotation from Wesley's above mentioned letters).

Lucidity of style, is, unfortunately, not conspicuous in A E F Dickinson's *The art of J S Bach* (Duckworth, 1936; revised edition Hinrichsen 1950). But because the book is illuminating, the small effort involved in reading some of his sentences more than once is well worth while. After a chapter on 'Bach the man', the author devotes the rest to the music, with chapters on the keyboard music, the organ works, orchestral and chamber music, and a very long chapter, in four section, on the choral music. Dickinson has also written *Bach's fugal works. With an account of fugue before and after Bach* (Pitman, 1956). Here he discusses in great detail this form as Bach used it in his choral works, as well as in those for organ and keyboard.

William Mann's *Introduction to the music of Johann Sebastian Bach* (Dobson, 1950) was designed 'to whet the appetite of the newcomer to Bach, to make him want to listen to, and better still to play, more of Bach's music'. Mann has certainly managed, within the limits of his seventy-five pages, to give a remarkable amount of information, though his list of the editions of the music is, inevitably, out of date.

Paul Hindemith's lecture *Johann Sebastian Bach: heritage and obligation* (Yale UP, 1952) is a somewhat provocative discussion of him as the man-in-the-street's composer, but none the less interesting as the view of a famous musician. A special aspect of Bach's music is studied in Norman Carrell's *Bach the borrower* (Allen & Unwin, 1967). Although the term 'borrow' is interpreted rather too literally—to include, for instance, all the chorale preludes by earlier composers which Bach set in his cantatas and elsewhere, including the organ preludes—the book has considerable value for the student. It brings together a mass of scattered information about what Bach re-used from both other composers and from himself. Here may be mentioned a significant book on a particular aspect of Bach's borrowings— Henry S Drinker's *The Bach chorale texts in English translation, with annotations showing the use of the melodies elsewhere by Bach in his vocal and organ works, with a musical index to the melodies* (Association of American Colleges, NY, 1941). Fundamental to the scholarly understanding of Bach is Robert Lewis Marshall's very important and beautifully printed *The compositional process of J S Bach. A study of the autograph scores and the vocal works* (2 vol, Princeton UP, 1972), which describes in great detail how he put the notes on paper.

VOCAL MUSIC

The Passions, Masses etc: Basil Smallman's *The background of passion music. J S Bach and his predecessors* (SCM Press, 1957; revised ed 1968; pb, BY, Dover, 1971) gives an admirable introduction to the subject, for it examines Bach's two Passions in detail in their historical context, showing them to be the culmination of a musical and liturgical tradition of great antiquity. As an adjunct, there should be mentioned a distinguished booklet by Sir Adrian Boult and Walter Emery, *The St Matthew Passion. Its preparation and performance* (Novello, 1949).

Terry has provided three excellent little guides (all in 'The musical pilgrim series), *Bach. The Magnificat, Lutheran Masses and Motets* (OUP, 1929; pb, NY, Johnson c1970), *Bach. The Passions* (OUP, 1926; NY Johnson c1970), and *Bach. The Mass in B minor* (OUP 1924; revised ed 1931; pb, NY, Johnson c1970). A forerunner of the last was his *Bach's Mass in B minor* (Maclehose, Glasgow, 1915).

Cantatas: The considerable literature on the cantatas begins with W G Whittaker's *Fugitive notes on certain cantatas and motets of J S Bach* (OUP 1924), dedicated to the Newcastle-upon-Tyne Bach Choir with whom, as also with a similar body at Glasgow, he performed in public the whole corpus of Bach's church and secular cantatas over a space of forty years. This is an immensely practical work of great value to conductors. Whittaker's much bigger two-volume work, *The cantatas of Johann Sebastian Bach, sacred and secular* (OUP, 1959) occupied him for many years, but its publication was delayed by his death in 1944. It was edited and revised by Harold Thompson, then head of music in the Scottish Region of the BBC. Whittaker was not able to take advantage of Alfred Dürr's radical redating of many of the cantatas. While it would have been impossible and undesirable to revise Whittaker's text to take account of the work of Dürr and other scholars, a foreword by the editor drawing attention to it would have been valuable. But the book as it stands is of enormous worth, shot through with a deep love and understanding of Bach.

Terry's *Bach. The cantatas and oratorios* (OUP, 1925; pb, NY, Johnson c1970) was intended only to furnish an introduction, which it does very well. It outlined the characteristics and purpose of the works, discussed the orchestra and accompaniment required. Despite his title, Terry did not touch on the oratorios. William Hannam's little book *Notes on the church cantatas of John Sebastian Bach* (OUP, 1928) has as its aim 'to state concisely the best and most authoritative

64

criticism of John Sebastian Bach's one hundred and ninety eight church cantatas, and to supplement it when necessary, and so to provide a handbook to the incomparable treasures of church music which they contain'. The authors he quotes are Forkel, Spitta, Parry, Schweitzer and Terry, and his references are to the Breitkopf and the Novello editions of the vocal scores. Sir Jack Westrup's *Bach cantatas* (BBC, 1966, 'BBC music guides') conveys a remarkable amount of information in its sixty pages about the nature and history of the church and secular cantatas, plotting their course from Mühlhausen to Leipzig. He makes illuminating comments on about twelve cantatas, with many passing references to others, and has some valuable pages about Bach's use of the orchestra.

The church cantatas of J S Bach, by Alec Robertson (Cassell, 1972), sets out the cantatas for Sundays and feast-days in the order of the Lutheran church year with details of the epistle and gospel. It also gives the scoring of each cantata, with notes on the musical style, and the source of the chorales.

It would be a penance for those who indulge in spiritual reading to be condemned to plough through the librettos Bach set, however acceptable they may have seemed to Lutherans of his time. Nevertheless, it is important to know something about the librettists of the church and secular cantatas, and this information is given in James Day's *The literary background to Bach's cantatas* (Dobson, 1961; pb, Dover, NY). The book would have been much more useful if the German texts frequently quoted had been translated into English. The complete definitive English texts are provided by Terry in his *Joh Seb Bach's cantata texts, sacred and secular. With a reconstruction of the Leipzig liturgy of his period* (Constable, 1926; Holland Press, 1964; Branden, Boston, 1973). Terry planned his translations to follow as nearly as possible Bach's declamation, but they are very free, and today the favoured method is that used by W G Whittaker and others, in which, though it makes deplorable English, the translation follows the order and, wherever possible, gives the equivalent of the German words.

General: There are three interesting American books which discuss some special cross-sections of Bach's vocal music. The title of Albert Riemenschneider's *Some aspects of the use of flutes in the sacred choral and vocal works of Johann Sebastian Bach* (Library of Congress, Washington DC, 1950) is self-explanatory. In *J S Bach as a biblical interpreter* (Princeton Theological Seminary, 1952), William H Scheide deals with the settings of texts drawn from the psalms, the prophets and the New Testament, adding a complete list of the principal ones. The author rather severely maintains that 'these works demand equal religious knowledge and religious scholarship', but much of his comment is illuminating. Bach used Gregorian chant in a number of chorales and elsewhere. The subject is discussed in a valuable book by Sister Mary J B Connor, *Gregorian chant and mediaeval hymn tunes in the works of J S Bach* (Catholic University of America Press, Washington, 1957). In 134 musical illustrations, placed at the end of the book, the author tabulates the plainsong melodies as they appear in the *Liber usualis*, with the Lutheran chorales taken or adapted from these, with Bach's use of them.

A useful pendant to the vocal music is provided by Miriam K Whaples's *Bach aria index* (Music Library Association, Ann Arbor, 1971). It is 'designed to help musicians find quickly all the Bach arias for whatever combination of voices and instruments may be available to them'. It is arranged by types of accompaniments and has an index of first lines.

INSTRUMENTAL MUSIC

Orchestral: C S Terry's *Bach's orchestra* (OUP 1932), while needing revision, remains the standard work. When reprinted in 1958, it had a foreword by Thurston Dart, who stuck his neck out in declaring that in spite of researches by scholars of the last thirty years, 'no part of Terry's masterly study (in his opinion) needs amending in the light of this more recent work'. In his postscript to the 1961 reprint, Professor Dart had, in part, to retract, acknowledging that many of Terry's conclusions

66

were rendered invalid by the gradual revision of the chronology of Bach's works, by the new approach to his use of various instruments, and by the fact that the *Neue Bach-Ausgabe* was under way.

Bach's Brandenburg Concertos (OUP, 1929) is the title of J A Fuller-Maitland's excellent short study in the 'Musical pilgrim' series, well suited to the average music-lover. More specialised is a longer work of the same title by Norman Carrell (Allen & Unwin, 1965). Besides analysing the music, it gives a wealth of information about the origins of the concertos, the survival of the material for performance, and the composition of the Margrave's small orchestra at Brandenburg and Leopold's larger one at Cöthen. The author discusses the precise nature of the various instruments required.

Organ works: A Eaglefield Hull compiled a 'catalogue raisonée', *Bach's organ works* (Musical Opinion, 1929), which is still useful as a means of quick reference. He gives the opening bars of each (for a prelude and fugue, each opening), with the page number of Bach Gesellschaft, Augener, Breitkopf, Novello, Peters Peters and Schirmer editions, and adds brief comments on each work. The introduction contains some technical notes and specifications of the organs Bach knew of or played on. Such information is also found in a number of the following books on the organ music, with details about registration and chronology—the latter different from what has become accepted in the last decade or so.

A good technical study is provided by André Pirro's *Johann Sebastian Bach. The organist and his works for organ* (Schirmer, NY, 1902), translated by Wallace Goodrich. Harvey Grace's *The organ works of Bach* (Novello, 1922) has remained a standard work. It is a delightfully readable book, full of perceptive comment and often spiced with wit. His smaller book, *The listener's guide to the organ music of Bach* (Columbia Gramophone Co, 1937), may also be recommended.

A longer study than Grace's book of 1922 is provided by Hermann Keller's *Bach's organ works. A contribution to their history, form, interpretation and performance,* translated from

the German by Helen Hewitt (Peters, NY, 1967). The author
provides each work with an analytical commentary and suggestions for performance, but divides the music into two groups
—free works and chorale compositions. While the book may be
recommended to students and teachers, they should be warned
that some of the author's chronology, especially for 'the last
great works of the Leipzig period' is of doubtful accuracy.
There are two excellent booklets by Walter Emery, in the series
'Notes on Bach's organ works (Novello)—*Eight short preludes
and fugues* (653-660) (1952) and *Six sonatas for two manuals
and pedal* (1957). These are companions to the revised edition
listed on p95, and provide searching analyses of all the problems that arise and are a mine of information.

Peter Williams's *Bach organ music* (one of the 'BBC music
guides', 1971) may be recommended as an admirable introduction, rich in insight about the relation of the instrument
and the music

Stainton de B Taylor's handbook *The chorale preludes of
J S Bach* (OUP, 1942) is another excellent book. His aim,
certainly achieved, is to widen the organist's acquaintance with
some of the sublimest music ever conceived for his instrument.
He first of all traces the origins and development of the form,
with special attention to the influence of Böhm, Pachelbel,
and Buxtehude on Bach, and follows with a chapter on the
performance of Bach's music. Another, and more original book,
on the same subject and called *The style of John Sebastian
Bach's chorale preludes*, by Robert L Tusler (University of
California Press, Berkeley, 1956) goes more deeply into the
fundamentals of Bach's style, not only in the chorale preludes
but in general. Tusler marvels at the balance he achieves between the vertical and the horizontal, that is the harmonic and
the contrapuntal. He has much of interest to say on the question of rhythm. 'What in essence', he asks, 'is the style of the
chorale prelude? It is Bach's treatment of rhythmic patterns
and melodic figures, marked by his power of unifying and
developing musical ideas. His great flights of fancy still remain
balanced and logical.' The only separate work on the

68

Orgelbüchlein is John E Hunt's *A companion to Bach's Orgel-büchlein* (Compton Organ Co, 1951), which is devoted mainly to performance and registration.

Style in performance is the subject of Robert Donington's *Tempo and rhythm in Bach's organ music* (Hinrichsen, 1960), a most stimulating little book, which is quite free of the jargon that sometimes accompanies such discussion. (His conclusions may be in part applied to the clavier works also.) He shows from Bach's very brief instruction in regard to tempo, quoted in Appendix 5 of vol 3 of Spitta, that the composer saw no useful purpose in listing detailed instructions in a matter than cannot be tied down to rules and measurements. 'The right tempo for a given piece of music', says Donington, 'is the tempo that fits, as the hand fits the glove, the interpretation of that piece *then being given* by the performer.' Another aspect of the complex performance problem is dealt with in Putnam Aldrich's *Ornamentation in J S Bach's organ works* (Coleman-Ross, NY, 1950).

The matter of the instrument is dealt with in an excellent article by William L Sumner 'The organ of Bach', in *Hinrichsen's eighth music book* (1956, reprinted 1966), pp18-135. This discusses: 1 organ music up to the time of Bach; 2 the German organ in his time; 3 his use of the organ; 4 the organs proved and played on by him; 5 the stops in his organs; 6 his music and the modern organ. In section 4 Sumner lists twenty-nine organs, adding notes below each specification about the builder, the date, the subsequent history of the instrument and Bach's association with it, and so forth. This information, collected from many sources, is not available elsewhere in this concise form, and the article is of great importance to organists and all who are interested in the instrument.

For clavier, general: The professional performer of the clavier works is, today, as likely to be a harpsichord or clavichord player as a pianist, but in any case both will need to know as much as possible about the difficult question of ornamentation. Walter Emery, one of the foremost English Bach scholars, provides an indispensable textbook *Bach's ornaments* (Novello, 1953, last reprinted 1974). Emery feels that Arnold Dolmetsch's *The interpretation of the music of the 17th and 18th centuries* (Novello, 1915; reprinted, University of Washington Press, Seattle, 1969), for long the standard work for English readers, gives the impression, perhaps not deliberately, that Bach's ornamentation can be reduced to a system which can be mastered without difficulty. Emery shows that it is a mistake to think of rules in view of the fact that very little is known about Bach's interpretations. He considers it 'unlikely that Bach always played his ornaments in exactly the same way', and he 'evidently regarded ornamentation as the business of the individual player'.

Rather wider in scope is Erwin Bodky's *The interpretation of Bach's keyboard works* (Harvard University Press; OUP, 1960). It includes chapters on the choice of instrument, the use of the modern piano, tempo, ornamentation, rhythmic conventions and symbolism. Although unequal and not reliable in every respect and therefore to be used with caution, it is a stimulating book for experienced readers.

The 'Well-tempered clavier' etc: Only a selection from the extensive literature on the '48' can be given here. There is an excellent 'Musical pilgrim' by J A Fuller-Maitland *The '48'. Bach's Wohltemperiertes Clavier* (OUP, 1925). Much more detailed is Stewart Macpherson's *A commentary on Book 1 (Book 2) of the forty-eight preludes and fugues of Johann Sebastian Bach* (Novello, 1934, 1937, 'Novello's music primers'). Macpherson, as I well know, having studied under him at the Royal Academy of Music, had a distinguished musical mind, and his analyses are thorough, perceptive and practical, and free of extra-musical associations.

Cecil Gray's *The forty-eight preludes and fugues of J S Bach* (OUP, 1938; pb 1971) is a most stimulating book. While he often allows himself a poetical interpretation of the music, his remarks deepen and widen one's knowledge of this miraculous work. He is particularly illuminating on the difference in style between book 1 and book 2.

Undoubtedly the most controversial book on the '48' is Fritz Rothschild's *A handbook to the performance of the 48 preludes and fugues of J S Bach according to the rules of the old tradition. Part 1: 1-24* (Black, 1956). In chapter two of an earlier book *The lost tradition in music* (Black, 1953; New York, Dufour, 1954), the same author had discussed the meaning of time-signatures as used by J S Bach, on the assumption that contemporary authorities proved that there were two speeds, one fast, the other slow, in common time, and that the determining factor was the particular combination of note-values in any given piece of music. This thesis was strongly contested by reviewers (see, for instance, Walter Emery, in *Music & letters*, July 1953, pp250-264). But, nothing daunted, Rothschild developed equally perverse ideas in his book on the '48', which again was strongly criticised by several scholars, among them Robert Donington, who said that Rothschild's hypothesis was not scholarship or musicianship, but fanaticism, and as such commanded respect, so long as one was not deceived into taking it at its face value. There remains another excellent 'Musical pilgrim' by J A Fuller-Maitland, *The keyboard suites of J S Bach* (OUP, 1925) which is the only separate book on the English and French suites, the partitas, and miscellaneous pieces.

Miscellaneous: Here may be conveniently grouped books about two great works, for the performance of which Bach did not specify, wholly or precisely, the instruments to be used. (The related editions are on pp128-9). Sir Donald Tovey's magisterial treatise *A companion to the Art of Fugue* (OUP, 1931) has become a standard work. A different approach is found in Mátyás Seiber's *The Art of Fugue. A guide to the new concert version by Walter Goehr and Mátyás Seiber* (LPO Booklets, 1944). The third, very important, book is H T David's *J S Bach's Musical Offering. History, interpretation and analysis* (Schirmer, NY, 1945).

Editions of Bach's music

The basis of the study of any composer's works is a thematic catalogue. Not all composers have been honoured in this way, but in the case of Bach there is a particularly fine example: *Thematisch-systematisches Verzeichnis der musikalischen Werke von Johann Sebastian Bach* (Leipzig, Breitkopf & Härtel, 1950). This was originally commissioned by the publishers in 1926, but did not appear until 1950. The first editors died at their task, but Wolfgang Schmieder took up the editorial work in 1937 and successfully completed his task thirteen years later, in spite of the destruction of the manuscript and all the proofs in an air raid on Leipzig in 1943. The opening bars of each movement of every work are given and bibliographical notes on each one. These notes sometimes run to three pages as, for example, in the case of the St Matthew Passion. They list manuscript sources, editions available, books and articles in all languages, and provide a wealth of other information. The arrangement is by form with the vocal works listed first.

The sequence of numbers in which Schmieder arranged his catalogue has now generally replaced the earlier system of identification based on the Bach-Gesellschaft volume number with the page reference. Schmieder's numbers are often preceded by the initials 'BWV', which stand for 'Bach Werke Verzeichnis', the sub-title of his catalogue. This is because he expressed reluctance to have 'S' for Schmieder used as in 'K' for Köchel in the case of Mozart, and over-modestly suggested 'BWV' instead. The numbers from Schmieder's catalogue have been used throughout this book to identify works, but in all cases where the number immediately precedes or follows a work's title neither the initials 'S' nor 'BWV' are used.

This very fine work represents one of the major contributions of the twentieth century to Bach scholarship. There was only one earlier attempt, in the previous century, based on the Bach-Gesellschaft edition mentioned below. The instrumental works were listed in *Thematisches Verzeichnis der Instrumentalwerke von Joh Seb Bach* edited by Alfred Dörffel, (Leipzig, Peters 1867; 2nd edition 1882). This listed the works divided into category by medium. The vocal works were arranged by form in *Thematisches Verzeichnis der Vocalwerke von Joh Seb Bach* edited by Carl Tamme (Leipzig, Peters, 1890). A concordance of numbers used in these indexes and in the Bach-Gesellschaft edition are provided in May de Forest Payne's *Melodic index to the works of Johann Sebastian Bach* (New York, Schirmer, 1935; 2nd edition New York, Peters, 1962). This fascinating book is a complete tabulation of the themes in Bach's works according to their melodic design, these themes being grouped according to the design formed by their first three intervals (repeated notes being ignored). The possible combinations of three intervals are divided into categories. The index includes 3,636 themes.

COLLECTED EDITIONS

The first complete edition of Bach's collected works was published under the auspices of the Bach Gesellschaft, founded in 1850, and was issued by Breitkopf and Härtel in 46 volumes and a supplement between 1851 and 1899. It has been reprinted 1947 (Ann Arbor), 1968 (Gregg Press) and in miniature score in 116 volumes (Kalmus). A fair number of items have been reprinted in Lea Pocket Scores and will be referred to below under the individual works.

On January 27 1900, the Bach-Gesellschaft was dissolved and the Neue Bach-Gesellschaft came into being, with the excellent idea of producing practical editions of the composer's works and arranging for performances throughout Germany. There had been inaccuracies in the standard edition, and the new publications, based on it, were far from trustworthy. The society's publication of an annual *Bach-Jahrbuch* began in 1904, containing the results of current scholarship, critical articles and reviews of books on Bach, was of real value and is still being produced today. An excellent account of the origins and antecedents of the Bach-Gesellschaft and of its successor, the Neue Bach-Gesellschaft is given by C S Terry in *Grove's dictionary of music and musicians* (Macmillan, 5th edition, 1954) under the heading 'Bach-Gesellschaft'.

For Bach, however, as for many other great composers of the past, editorial standards have changed radically in the first part of the twentieth century, so that as the second centenary of his death approached, it was felt that a new complete edition was required. Thus the celebrations in 1950 were followed in 1954 by the beginning of the *Neue Bach Ausgabe* (New Bach edition) under the general editorial supervision of the Johann Sebastian Bach Institut, Göttingen, and the Bach Archiv, Leipzig. It is divided into seven series and a supplement, in which the following volumes, mostly with separate textual commentary in German, have so far been issued by Bärenreiter.

Series 1: Cantatas (Arranged according to the liturgical calendar)
Vol 1. Advent cantatas. 61, 36, 62, 132 (Alfred Dürr, Werner Neumann).
Vol 2. Cantatas for the 1st day of Christmas. 63, 197a, 110, 91, 191 (Dürr).
Vol 4. Cantatas for the New Year and the Sunday after New Year. 190, 41, 16, 171, 143, 153 (Neumann).
Vol 5. Cantatas for Epiphany and 1st and 2nd Sundays after Epiphany. 65, 123, 154, 124, 32, 155, 3, 13 (Marianne Helms).
Vol 7. Cantatas for Septuagesima and Sexagesima. 144, 84, 92, 18, 181, 126 (Neumann).

Vol 10.   Cantatas for the 2nd and 3rd days of Easter.   66, 6, 134, 145, 158 (Dürr).

Vol 12.   Cantatas for Cantate until Exaudi.   166, 108, 86, 87, 37, 128, 43, 44, 183 (Dürr).

Vol 13.   Cantatas for the 1st day of Whitsun.   172, 59, 74, 34 (Dietrich Kilian).

Vol 14.   Cantatas for the 2nd and 3rd days of Whitsun. 173, 68, 174, 184, 175 (Dürr, Arthur Mendel).

Vol 15.   Cantatas for Trinity and the 1st Sunday after Trinity.   165, 194, 176, 129, 75, 20, 39 (Dürr, Robert Freeman, James Webster).

Vol 18.   Cantatas for the 7th and 8th Sundays after Trinity. 54, 186, 107, 187, 136, 178, 45 (Dürr, Leo Treitler).

Vol 21.   Cantatas for the 13th and 14th Sundays after Trinity.   77, 33, 164, 25, 78, 17 (Neumann).

Vol 27.   Cantatas for the 24th to the 27th Sundays after Trinity.   60, 26, 90, 116, 70, 140 (Dürr).

Vol 30.   Cantatas for Michaelmas.   130, 19, 149, 50 (Helms).

Vol 33.   Wedding cantatas.   196, 34a, 120a, 197, 195 (Frederick Hudson).

Vol 35.   Homage cantatas for Weimar, Weissenfels & Köthen. 208, 134a, 173a (Dürr).

Vol 36.   Homage cantatas in honour of the Electoral House of Saxony I.   213, 214, 206 (Neumann).

Vol 37.   Homage cantatas in honour of the Electoral House of Saxony II.   207a, 215 (Neumann).

Vol 38.   Festival cantatas for Leipzig University ceremonies. 205, 207, 198, 36b (Neumann).

Vol 39.   Birthday and secular cantatas.   36c, 30a, 210a, 212 (Neumann).

Vol 40.   Wedding cantatas and secular cantatas.   202, 216, 210, 204, 201, 211 (Neumann).

Series II: Masses, Passions and Oratorios

Vol 1.   Mass in B minor.   232 (Friedrich Smend).

Vol 3.   Magnificat.   243a, 243 (Dürr).

Vol 4.   St John Passion.   245 (Mendel).

Vol 5.   St Matthew Passion.   244 (Dürr).

Vol 5a. St Matthew Passion early version. 244b (Dürr).

Vol 6. Christmas Oratorio. 248 (Walter Blankenburg, (Dürr).

Series III: Motets, Chorales and Songs

Vol 1. Motets. 225-230, 118 (Konrad Ameln).

Series IV: Organ works

Vol 2. Organ Chorale Preludes of the Leipzig Autograph (the Eighteen and the Canonic Variations). 651-668, 651a-656a, 658a-668a, 769a (Hans Klotz).

Vol 3. Miscellaneous Organ Chorales. 690, 691, 694-701, 703, 704, 706, 709-715, 717, 718, 720-722, 724-738, 741, 722a, 729a, 732a, 735a, 738a, O Lamm Gottes unschuldig (Klotz).

Vol 4. Clavierübung part 3. 552 (Prelude and fugue E flat major), 669-689, 802-5 (Manfred Tessmer).

Vol 5. Preludes, Fantasias, Toccatas and Fugues I. 531, 545, 547, 549, 546, 537, 562, 532, 539, 538, 533, 548, 540, 534, 550, 541, 535, 542, 536, 543, 544 (Kilian).

Vol 6. Preludes, Fantasias, Toccatas and Fugues II. 564, 570, 573-575, 565, 566, 568, 578, 569, 551, 563, 579, 545a, 574a, b, 532a, 549a, 533a, 535a, 536a, 543a (Kilian).

Series V: Keyboard and Lute Works

Vol 3. Inventions and symphonies. 772-801 (Georg von Dadelsen).

Vol 4. Clavierbüchlein for Anna Magdalena Bach. 82, 299, 508-518, 515a, 573, 691, 728, 812-816, 827, 830, 841, 846/1, 988/1, 991, 817, App. 113-116, 117a, 117b, 118-132, 183 (Dadelsen).

Vol 5. Clavierbüchlein for Wilhelm Friedemann Bach. 691, 772-801, 824, 836, 837, 841-843, 846a, 847-851, 853, 854, 855a, 856, 857, 924, 924a, 925-932, 953, 994 (Wolfgang Plath).

Series VI: Chamber music works

Vol 1. Works for violin. 1001-6, 1021, 1023, 1014-19 (Günter Hausswald, Rudolf Gerber).

Vol 3. Works for flute. 1034, 1035, 1030, 1032, 1039, 1013 (Hans-Peter Schmitz).

Series VI: Orchestral works
 Vol 1. Orchestral suites. 1066-69 (Heinrich Besseler).
 Vol 2. Six Brandenburg Concertos 1046-31 and original version of concerto no 1 (Besseler).
 Vol 2. Supplement. Early version of concerto 5 (Dürr).
 Vol 6. Concertos for 3 and 4 harpsichords 1063-5 (Rudolf Edler and Karl Heller).
 Vol 7. Various solo concertos reconstructed. 1052, 1055, 1056, 1060, 1064 (Wilfred Fischer).
Series VIII
 Vol 1. Canons 1072-8, Musical Offering 1079 (Christoph Wolff).
Supplement: (Documents in German)
 Vol 1. Letters and documents of J S Bach (Neumann, Hans-Joachim Schulze).
 Vol 2. Writings and printed documents on the life of J S Bach (Neumann and Schulze).
 Vol 3. Writings and documents 1750-1880.

The aim of this indispensable edition, which follows the original sources faithfully, is to present each work in an authentic text, giving the alternative versions and revision when appropriate. Bärenreiter also issue miniature scores, which are listed below under each work, and some performing material, based on the edition.

OTHER EDITIONS

All editions are in score unless otherwise stated, and the word 'by' is here equivalent to 'edited by' or 'arranged by'. Publishers names are given in full except for the following:
 Bä = Bärenreiter
 B&H = Breitkopf and Härtel
 Eul = Eulenburg
 LPS = Lea Pocket Scores
 Nov = Novello

OUP = Oxford University Press
UE = Universal Edition

When no town is given the place of publication is London. The place of publication and the editor's initials are omitted when either recurs several times in succession. Publishers' addresses are most readily available in the *British catalogue of music* (issued by the Bibliographical Services Division of the British Library), which is to be found in major public libraries throughout the world. Besides the addresses of all British music publishers, this catalogue includes those of the leading American firms and of many European firms which have branches in London.

The following lists are not meant to be exhaustive, as the number of editions of Bach's music is immense, and the mere listing of them would require a much larger book than the present one. The general principles of selection may be outlined as follows: scholarly quality and the consequent value of the text or editorial preface or of both; the historical interest of the editor or arranger as a famous performer or teacher; the fact that a work (for example, the vocal score of a mass) may not have been otherwise issued in that form; the interest of an arrangement, in an unusual but convenient medium. In addition to well-edited pocket or miniature scores, other useful ones without editor's name have also been included.

It cannot be too strongly emphasised that the presence of a title in these lists is not necessarily an indication that it is in print at the time of writing. Even recent editions seem to go out of print almost overnight, and in the case of anything issued before the end of the second world war the chances are that it may not be available for purchase. In such a case the reader is recommended to try his local public library.

One problem which may be special to Bach is that a vast number of extracts, selections and arrangements have been made from his music, due to its nature and its wealth of melody. The cantatas, the oratorios, the chorale settings—to mention only these three categories—contain numerous beautiful pieces which are easily separable and can be performed in isolation.

Only a few are mentioned below, generally because of the personal eminence of the arranger or editor.

Bach's music also lends itself to the creation of popular composite works, drawn from both vocal and instrumental originals. Such, for example, is the ballet *The wise virgins*, compiled by Sir William Walton, from which there are a suite, the ever-fresh excerpt 'Sheep may safely graze' and 'Ah how ephemeral' (arranged for two pianos by Walter Goehr), all issued by OUP. The same firm publishes an anthology of an unusual type *A Bach book for Harriet Cohen*, which consists of piano versions of various pieces made by a dozen eminent musicians, including Bax, Bliss, Vaughan Williams and Walton. Such publications as this lie rather outside the mainstream of this section of the present book.

The categories in which editions are grouped in the following selective lists are those of the *Neue Bach Ausgabe*, with some modification here and there. The sequence is, first, vocal music, followed by instrumental music and, finally, orchestral music.

Vocal music   CANTATAS

By far the most extensive group of Bach's work comprises the cantatas, the majority of which were composed for church use and only some fifteen for secular occasions. For over seventy years after Bach's death they were completely forgotten. Their revival began in Germany from the late 1820s onwards, after Mendelssohn's epoch-making performance of the St Matthew Passion had made the public aware of Bach's greatness.

The church cantatas contain some of Bach's most deeply felt and wonderfully wrought vocal music. Their chronology has been thoroughly investigated at the Bach Institute at Göttingen by Alfred Dürr and other German scholars, with the result that much previous dating, based largely on Spitta, has had to be revised. Their findings were first published in the *Bach Jahrbuch* for 1957 and were summarised in an article 'New light on Bach', which Dürr contributed to the *Musical times* for June 1966. It is of absorbing interest. The findings show, for instance, that the great majority of the Leipzig cantatas date from between 1723 and 1729, and that most of the so-called 'late' chorale cantatas were written in 1724 and 1725.

Apart from the as yet incomplete *Neue Bach Ausgabe* the most important set of the cantatas, apart from 214 and 216, is published by Breitkopf & Härtel in full score, vocal score, choral score and choral parts. Seventy-three of the vocal scores have English translations, and these are noted under the individual cantatas below. The earlier issues of the vocal scores gave no indication of the instrumentation at all, later ones placed it beside the first piano stave in each movement, and the latest issues (1966) show the instrumentation at the start as above, but in addition give it at many points in the course of choruses and arias. Breitkopf issue a useful catalogue of their edition, with details of the scoring and approximate timings of each work.

    1   Wie schön leuchtet der Morgenstern miniature score by Arnold Schering (Eul), vocal score with English translation (B&H), vocal score by J E West with English translation by P England (Nov).

    2   Ach Gott vom Himmel sieh' darein vocal score with English translation (B&H).

    4   Christ lag in Todesbanden miniature score by Schering (Eul), sinfonia, chorale and variation, organ solo by E Power Biggs (H W Gray, New York), vocal score by West with English translation by England (Nov).

    6   Bleib' bei uns, denn es will Abend werden miniature scores (Bä) and by Schering (Eul), vocal score with English translation (B&H), score and choral score by Paul Horn (Hänssler/Nov), vocal score with English translation by J Troutbeck (Nov).

    7   Christ unser Herr zum Jordan kam miniature score by Schering (Eul), vocal score with English translation (B&H).

    8   Liebster Gott, wann werd' ich sterben? miniature score by Schering (Eul), vocal score with English translation (B&H), vocal score with English translation by J Troutbeck (Nov).

10   *Meine Seel' erhebt den Herren* by Paul Steinitz with English translation (Curwen; Schirmer, New York), vocal score with English translation (B&H).

11   *Lobet Gott in seinen Reichen* miniature score by Schering (Eul), vocal score by West with English translation by England (Nov), score and choral score by Horn (Hänssler/Nov).

12   *Weinen, Klagen, Sorgen, Zagen* miniature score by Schering (Eul), vocal score with English translation (B&H), vocal score by West with English translation by England (Nov).

14   *Wär' Gott nicht mit uns diese Zeit* Facsimile of autograph of vocal parts (Deutscher Verlag für Musik, Leipzig).

17   *Wer Dank opfert, der preiset mich* miniature score with English translation (Eul) score and choral score by Hans Grischkat (Hänssler/Nov), vocal score by West with English translation by W G Rothsay (Nov), by W G Whittaker with English words by C S Terry (OUP).

18   *Gleich wie der Regen und Schnee vom Himmel fällt* miniature score (Bä), sinfonia by Whittaker (OUP), vocal score with English translation (B&H).

19   *Es erhub sich ein Streit* miniature score by Schering (Eul).

20   *O Ewigkeit, du Donnerwort* miniature score by Schering (Eul).

21   *Ich hatte viel Bekümmernis* miniature score by Schering (Eul), vocal score by G Rösler (Peters), vocal score with English translation by Troutbeck (Nov), with English translation (B&H), by Ifor Jones with English translation by Jones and J M Stein (Schirmer, New York).

22   *Jesus nahm zu sich die Zwölfe* vocal score by Whittaker with English translation by Terry (OUP). 'Humble us by Thy Goodness', arranged for piano and piano duet by Harriet Cohen (OUP), for two pianos by Becket Williams (OUP), for strings by Reginald Jacques (OUP), and for organ by Desmond Ratcliffe (Nov).

23   *Du wahrer Gott und Davids Sohn* score and choral score by Grischkat (Hänssler/Nov), vocal score with English translation (B&H).

25   *Es ist nichts Gesundes an meinem Leibe* vocal score
by Whittaker with English translation by Terry (Stainer & Bell),
and by West with English translation by Troutbeck (Nov).

26   *Ach wie flüchtig, ach wie nichtig* vocal score with
English translation (B&H).

27   *Wer Weiss, wie nahe mir mein Ende* miniature score
with English translation (Eul) score and choral score by Grischkat (Hänssler/Nov), vocal score by West with English translation
by Troutbeck (Nov), vocal score with English translation (B&H).

28   *Gottlob! Nun geht das Jahr zu Ende* miniature score
by Grischkat with English translation (Eul) vocal score by J
Pointer with English translation by W G Rothsay (Nov).

29   *Wir danken dir Gott, wir danken dir* miniature score
with English translation (Eul) score and choral score by Grischkat (Hänssler/Nov), vocal score with English translation (B&H),
sinfonia by Whittaker (OUP).

30   *Freue dich, erlöste Schar* vocal score with English
translation (B&H).

31   *Der Himmel lacht, die Erde jubilieret* miniature score
by Schering (Eul), vocal scores by Whittaker with English translation by Terry (OUP)/with English translation by Henry
Drinker (Schirmer, New York).

32   *Liebster Jesu, mein Verlangen* score and choral score
by Grischkat (Hänssler/Nov), vocal score with English translation (B&H).

34   *O ewiges Feuer, O Ursprung der Liebe* miniature
scores (Bä) and by Schering (Eul), score and choral score by
Schuberth (Hänssler/Nov), vocal score with English translation
by Troutbeck (Nov), vocal score with English translation (B&H).

35   *Geist und Seele wird verwirret*, sinfonia 1 and 2 by
Whittaker (OUP), sinfonia 1 for 2 pianos by Walter Emery
(Nov).

36   *Schwingt freudig euch empor* miniature score (Bä).

37   *Wer da glaubet und getauft wird* miniature score with
English translation (Eul) score and choral score by Grischkat
(Hänssler/Nov), vocal score with English translation (B&H).

38   Aus tiefer Not schrei' ich zu dir miniature score with English translation (Eul), vocal score by West with English translation by England (Nov), vocal score with English translation (B&H).

39   Brich dem Hungrigen dein Brot miniature score by Schering (Eul), vocal score by West with English translation by England (Nov), vocal score with English translation (B&H).

40   Dazu ist erschienen der Sohn Gottes vocal score with English translation (B&H).

41   Jesu, nun sei gepreiset vocal score with English translation by Troutbeck (Nov).

43   Gott fahret auf mit Jauchzen vocal score by R Franz with English translation by W H Millman (Nov).

44   Sie werden euch in den Bann tun vocal score with English translation (B&H).

45   Es ist dir gesagt, Mensch, was gut ist miniature score (Bä).

46   Schauet doch und sehet, ob irgend ein Schmerz sei miniature score by Schering (Eul), vocal score by West with English translation by England (Nov), vocal score with English translation (B&H), score and choral score by Horn (Hänssler/Nov).

48   Ich elender Mensch, wer wird mich erlösen vocal score with English translation (B&H).

50   Nun ist das Heil und die Kraft miniature score by Schering (Eul), score and choral score by Horn (Hänssler/Nov), vocal score with English translation by Troutbeck (Nov), vocal score with English translation (B&H), vocal score by Whittaker with English translation by Terry (OUP).

51   Jauchzet Gott in allen Landen miniature score by Schering (Eul), vocal score with English translation (B&H), score by Horn (Hänssler/Nov).

53   Schlage doch, gewünschte Stunde miniature score (Eul, also Ricordi), vocal score for unison voices by Whittaker (OUP), vocal scores with English translation (B&H), by Pointer with English translation by England (Nov).

54 *Widerstehe doch der Sünde* miniature score by Schering (Eul).

55 *Ich armer Mensch, ich Sündenknecht* miniature score by Schering (Eul), vocal score with English translation (B&H).

56 *Ich will den Kreuzstab gerne tragen* miniature score by Schering (Eul) and with no editor (Ricordi), facsimile of autograph (Drei Masken Verlag, Munich), vocal score by Melville Cook with English translation by H S Drinker (Peters), vocal score with English translation (B&H).

57 *Selig ist der Mann* vocal score with English translation (B&H).

59 *Wer mich liebet, der wird mein Wort halten* miniature score (Bä).

60 *O Ewigkeit, du Donnerwort* miniature score by Schering (Eul).

61 *Nun komm, der Heiden Heiland* miniature score (Bä), miniature score with English translation (Eul) score and choral score by Grischkat (Hänssler/Nov), vocal score by Ivor Atkins with English translation by R M Craster (Nov).

62 *Nun komm, der Heiden Heiland* miniature score (Bä), miniature score with English translation (Eul) full score and choral score by Grischkat (Hänssler/Nov).

63 *Christen, ätzet diesen Tag* miniature score (Bä) vocal score by West, with English translation by C Aveling (Nov), vocal score with English translation (B&H).

64 *Sehet, welch eine Liebe hat uns der Vater erzeiget* vocal score by Whittaker with English translation by Terry (OUP), vocal score with English translation (B&H).

65 *Sie werden aus Saba alle kommen* miniature score by Schering (Eul), score and choral score by Horn (Hänssler/ Nov), vocal score by Pointer, English translation by England (Nov).

67 *Halt im Gedächtnis Jesum Christ* miniature score by Schering (Eul), vocal score by Pointer, English translation by Terry (Nov), vocal score with English translation (B&H).

68 *Also hat Gott die Welt geliebt* miniature score (Bä), miniature score (Eul) score and choral score by Grischkat

(Hänssler/Nov), vocal score with English translation by Troutbeck (Nov), vocal score with English translation (B&H).

69   *Lobe den Herrn, meine Seele* vocal score with English
translation (B&H).

70   *Wachtet, betet, seid bereit allezeit* vocal score by E
H Thorne with English translation by C Aveling (Nov).

71   *Gott ist mein König* facsimile of autograph (Deutscher
Verlag für Musik, Leipzig), vocal score with English translation
(B&H).

72   *Alles nur nach Gottes Willen* vocal score with English
translation (B&H).

73   *Herr, wie du willt, so schick's mit mir* vocal score with
English translation (B&H).

75   *Die Elenden sollen essen* sinfonia by Whittaker (OUP),
for two pianos by Emery (Nov), 'Mein Herze glaubt' for piano
by Herbert Murrill (OUP).

76   *Die Himmel erzählen die Ehre Gottes* vocal score with
English translation (B&H), sinfonia by Whittaker (OUP).

78   *Jesu, der du meine Seele* miniature score (Bä), and by
Schering (Eul), full and choral score by Horn (Hänssler/Nov),
vocal score with English translation (B&H).

79   *Gott, der Herr, ist Sonn' und Schild* miniature score
by Schering (Eul) score and choral score by Horn (Hänssler/
Nov), vocal score by Atkins with English translation by M E
Butler (Nov), vocal score with English translation (B&H).

80   *Ein feste Burg ist unser Gott* miniature score by Schering (Eul) score and choral score by Horn (Hänssler/Nov), score
by Rösler (Peters), vocal score with English translation by Troutbeck (Nov), vocal score with English translation (B&H).

81   *Jesus schläft, was soll ich hoffen* miniature score by
Schering (Eul), vocal score by Atkins with English translation
by M E Butler (Nov).

82   *Ich habe genug* vocal score with English translation
(B&H), miniature score (LPS).

83   *Erfreute Zeit im neuen Bunde* miniature score (LPS).

84   *Ich bin vergnügt mit meinem Glücke* miniature score
(LPS).

85   *Ich bin ein guter Hirt* miniature scores by Schering (EUL), no editor (Ricordi), no editor (LPS).

91   *Gelobet seist du, Jesu Christ* miniature score (Bä).

92   *Ich hab in Gottes Herz und Sinn* miniature score by Schering (Eul).

93   *Wer nur den lieben Gott lässt walten* miniature score with English translation by Grischkat (Eul), by Max Reger (Bote & Bock, Berlin), vocal score by Pointer with English translation by Troutbeck (Nov).

95   *Christus, der ist mein Leben* vocal score by West with English translation by Aveling (Nov), vocal score with English translation (B&H).

98   *Was Gott tut, das ist wohlgetan* vocal score by Whittaker, English translation by Terry (OUP).

102   *Herr, deine Augen sehen nach dem Glauben* vocal score with English translation (B&H).

104   *Du Hirte Israel, höre* miniature score by Siegfried Ochs (Eul), vocal score with English translation by Troutbeck (Nov), full and choral score by Horn (Hänssler/Nov).

105   *Herr, gehe nicht ins Gericht* miniature score by Schering (Eul) score and choral score by Horn (Hänssler/Nov), vocal score by Whittaker with English translation by Terry (OUP).

106   *Gottes Zeit ist die allerbeste Zeit* miniature score by Schering (Eul), vocal score with English translation by Troutbeck (Nov), vocal score with English translation (B&H), sonatina for piano by James Friskin (Fischer, Glen Rock, NY).

107   *Was willst du dich betrüben* vocal score by Whittaker with English translation by Terry (OUP).

108   *Es ist euch gut, dass ich hingehe* miniature score by Dürr (Bä).

110   *Unser Mund sei voll Lachens* miniature score by Dürr (Bä).

112   *Der Herr ist mein getreuer Hirt* vocal score by Pointer with English translation by England (Nov), vocal score with English translation (B&H).

115   *Mache dich, mein Geist bereit* vocal score by Atkins with English translation by Terry (OUP).

116   Du Friedefürst, Herr Jesu Christ vocal score with English translation (B&H).

117   Sei Lob und Ehr' dem höchsten Gut vocal score with English translation (B&H).

118   O Jesu Christ, mein's Lebens Licht vocal scores by Emil Kahn with English translation by Elizabeth Kulka (Marks Music, New York), by E S Roper with English translation by Colles (OUP), with English translation (B&H), by Ifor Jones with English translation by Jones and J M Stein (Schirmer, New York).

119   Preise, Jerusalem, den Herrn miniature score by Schering (Eul), vocal score by West with English translation by England (Nov).

120   Gott, man lobet dich in der Stille vocal score with English translation (B&H).

121   Christum wir sollen loben schon vocal score by Whittaker with English translation by Terry (OUP).

122   Das neugebor'ne Kindelein vocal score with English translation (B&H), and, with choral parts, by W G Whittaker, English translation by Terry (OUP).

123   Liebster Immanuel, Herzog der Frommen miniature score by Schering (Eul).

124   Meinen Jesum lass' ich nicht vocal score with English translation (B&H).

127   Herr Jesu Christ, wahr'r Mensch und Gott miniature score (Eul) score and choral score by Grischkat (Hänssler/Nov), vocal score with English translation (B&H).

128   Auf Christi Himmelfahrt allein miniature score by Dürr (Bä).

131   Aus der Tiefe rufe ich, Herr, zu dir miniature score with English translation (Eul) score and choral score by Grischkat (Hänssler), vocal score with English translation (B&H), miniature score (LPS).

132   Bereitet die Wege, bereitet die Bahn miniature scores by Dürr and Neumann (Bä), no editor (LPS).

133   Ich freue mich in dir miniature score (LPS), vocal score with English translation (B&H).

134   Ein Herz, das seinen Jesum lebend weiss miniature score by Dürr (Bä).

135   Ach Herr, mich armen Sünder facsimile of autograph (Röder, Leipzig).

137   Lobe den Herren, den mächtigen König der Ehren miniature score with English translation (Eul), score and choral score by Grischkat (Hänssler/ Nov), vocal score with English translation (B&H), miniature score (LPS).

138   Warum betrübst du dich, mein Herz? miniature score (LPS).

139   Wohl dem, der sich auf seinen Gott miniature score (LPS).

140   Wachtet auf, ruft uns die Stimme miniature scores (LPS), by Schering (Eul) and by Whittaker (OUP), score and choral score by Horn (Hänssler/Nov), vocal scores by Whittaker (OUP) with English translation (B&H) by E Prout with English translation by Troutbeck (Nov); for cello and piano by William Alwyn with violin and viola parts by Watson Forbes (OUP); for two pianos by Whittaker (OUP); chorale prelude transcribed for orchestra by Eugene Ormandy (Boosey & Hawkes).

141   Das ist je gewisslich wahr miniature score (LPS).

142   Uns ist ein Kind geboren miniature score (LPS), vocal score by Walter Ehret (Piedmont music, New York); aria 'Thy birthday is come' by Mary Howe for two pianos (OUP).

144   Nimm, was dein ist miniature score by Neumann (Bä), vocal score by Whittaker with English translation by Terry (OUP).

146   Wir Müssen durch viel Trübsal miniature score (LPS).

147   Herz und Mund und Tat und Leben miniature score (LPS), vocal score by William Goldsworthy (H W Gray, New York); 'Jesu, joy of man's desiring' for piano by Leonard Borwick (OUP), and Myra Hess (OUP), vocal parts by Sir Hugh Allen (OUP), for strings by Reginald Jacques (OUP).

149   Man singet mit Freuden vocal score by Pointer with English translation by England (Nov).

150   Nach dir, Herr, verlanget mich vocal score with English translation (B&H).

151 *Süsser Trost, mein Jesu kommt* full and choral score by D Hellman (Hänssler/Nov), miniature scores (LPS), by Vittorio Gui (Boosey & Hawkes), vocal score with English translation (B&H).

152 *Tritt auf die Glaubensbahn* miniature score (LPS), vocal scores by C K Scott with English translation by B E Bulman (OUP), by Günter Raphael with English translation by F P Copeland (B&H) with English translation (B&H), by E H Hunt (Schott).

153 *Schau, lieber Gott, wie meine Feind'* miniature score (LPS).

154 *Mein liebster Jesus ist verloren* miniature score (LPS).

155 *Mein Gott, wie lang', ach lange* score and choral score by Horn (Hänssler/Nov), miniature score (LPS), vocal score with English translation (B&H); 'Wirf, mein Herz' for one and two pianos by Harriet Cohen (OUP).

156 *Ich steh' mit einem Fuss im Grabe* miniature score (LPS).

157 *Ich lasse dich nicht* miniature score (LPS).

158 *Der Friede sei mit dir* miniature scores by Dürr (Bä), by Grischkat with English translation (Eul), no editor (LPS), full and choral score by Grischkat (Hänssler/Nov).

159 *Sehet, wir geh'n hinauf gen Jerusalem* miniature score with English translation score and vocal score by Grischkat (Hänssler/Nov), miniature score (LPS), vocal score with English translation (B&H).

160 *Ich weiss, dass mein Erlöser lebt* miniature score (LPS), vocal score with English translation (B&H).

161 *Komm, du süsse Todesstunde* miniature score by Schering (Eul), no editor (LPS), vocal score with English translation (B&H), by Vittorio Gui with English translation by H S Drinker (Boosey & Hawkes), vocal score by C K Scott with English translation by B E Bulman (OUP).

162 *Ach, ich sehe, itzt, da ich zur Hochzeit gehe* miniature score (LPS).

163 *Nur Jedem das Seine* miniature score (LPS).

164 *Ihr, die ihr euch von Christo nennet* miniature score (LPS).

165   *O heil'ges Geist- und Wasserbad* aria 'Jesu, der aus grosser Liebe' by Michael Tippett and Walter Bergmann (Schott).

166   *Wo gehest du hin?* miniature score by Dürr (Bä).

168   *Tue Rechnung! Donnerwort* miniature score (LPS).

169   *Gott soll allein mein Herze haben* niniature score (LPS) vocal score with English translation (B&H).

170   *Vergnügte Ruh', beliebte Seelenlust* miniature score (LPS), by Gui with English translation by Drinker (Boosey & Hawkes), vocal score with English translation (B&H).

171   *Gott, wie dein Name, so ist auch dein Ruhm* vocal score with English translation (B&H).

172   *Erschallet, ihr Lieder* miniature score by Dietrich Kilian (Bä).

175   *Er rufet seinen Schafen mit Namen* miniature score by Dürr and Arthur Mendel (Bä).

176   *Es ist ein trotzig und verzagt Ding* miniature score by Dürr, Robert Freeman and James Webster (Bä), miniature score by Schering (Eul) full and choral score by Horn (Hänssler/Nov).

180   *Schmücke dich, o liebe Seele* vocal score by West with English translation by A H Fox-Strangways (Nov), vocal score with English translation (B&H).

182   *Himmelskönig, sei willkommen* miniature score by Schering (Eul), vocal score with English translation by Whittaker (OUP).

183   *Sie werden euch in den Bann tun* miniature score (LPS).

184   *Erwünschtes Freudenlicht* miniature score (LPS).

185   *Barmherziges Herze der ewigen Liebe* miniature score (LPS).

186   *Ärgre dich, o Seele, nicht* full and choral score by Hellmann (Hänssler/Nov).

188   *Ich habe mein Zuversicht* miniature score (LPS).

189   *Meine Seele rühmt und preist* miniature score (LPS).

191   *Gloria in excelsis Deo* vocal score, no editor, (Schirmer, New York).

198   *Lass Fürstin, lass noch einen Strahl* vocal score with English translation (B&H).

199   *Mein Herze schwimmt im Blut* vocal score with English translation (B&H).

200   *Bekennen will ich seinen Namen* (fragmentary) by Ludwig Landshoff (Peters).

201   *Geschwinde, geschwinde, ihr wirbelnden Winde* miniature score (LPS), vocal score by West with English translation by J M Diack (Nov).

202   *Weichet nur, betrübte Schatten* miniature score (LPS).

203   *Amore traditore* by Michael Tippett and Walter Bergmann (Schott), miniature score (LPS).

204   *Ich bin in mir vergnügt* miniature score (LPS).

205   *Zerreisset, zersprenget, zertrümmert die Gruft* miniature score by Schering (Eul).

207   *Vereinigte Zwietracht der wechselnden Saiten* miniature score by Neumann (Bä), vocal score by Stewart Wilson (OUP).

208   *Was mir behagt* miniature score by Dürr (Bä), orchestrated by L Stokowski (Peters), vocal score no editor with English translation by Stewart Robb (Schirmer, New York); 'Schafe können sicher weiden', one of Bach's most popular airs, apparently first arranged by J M Diack (Paterson, 1929), then orchestrated by Percy Grainger (Schirmer, New York, 1932) under the title 'Blithe bells'; thereafter translation as 'Sheep may safely graze' and other versions in innumerable other arrangements, *eg* as part song 'Flocks may graze in tranquil safety' by H A Chambers (Nov), for piano by Egon Petri (Boosey & Hawkes), and by Dinu Lipatti (Schott), for two pianos by Mary Howe (OUP), for SATB 'Flocks by shepherd safe attended' by Maurice Jacobson (Curwen), for soprano, recorders and continuo by Hunt (Schott).

210   *O holder Tag, erwünschte Zeit* facsimile of autograph (Deutscher Verlag für Musik, Leipzig).

211   *Schweiget stille, plaudert nicht* facsimiles of autograph (Wiener Philharmonischer Verlag, and Deutscher Verlag für Musik, Leipzig), miniature scores by Schering (Eul), no editor (Ricordi), by Terry (Stainer & Bell), vocal score by H E Baker with English translation by J M Diack (Paterson).

212 *Mer Hahn en neue Oberkeet* facsimile of autograph (Henle), miniature score by Max Albert (Eul), vocal scores by Whittaker (OUP), by Neumann (Peters), by Baker with English translation by Diack (Paterson).

213 *Lasst uns sorgen, lasst uns wachen* miniature score by Neumann (Bä).

214 *Tönet, ihr Pauken! Erschallet, Trompeten!* Miniature score by Neumann (Bä).

216 *Vergnügte Pleissen-Stadt* (fragmentary) vocal score by Werner Wolffheim completed by Georg Schumann with English translation by Terry (Lienau, Berlin).

MASSES, PASSIONS AND ORATORIOS

Mass in B minor (232) facsimile of the autograph (Insel-Verlag, 1924) miniature scores by Friedrich Smend (Bä) Fritz Vollbach (Eul), vocal scores by Rösler (Peters) no editor (Nov).

Mass in F major (233), Mass in A major (234), Mass in G minor (235), Mass in G major (236), scores and vocal scores by Lothar Hoffmann-Erbrecht (Peters).

Magnificat D major and E flat major (243 and 243a) miniature scores by Dürr (Bä), D major Schering (Eul), score by K Straube (Peters), vocal scores by H Roth (Peters), with English translation by Troutbeck (Nov).

Magnificat D major with Christmas interpolations miniature score (LPS).

Kleines Magnificat (Anh 21) full score by Hellmann (Hänssler/Nov).

St Matthew Passion (244) facsimiles of the autograph (Insel-Verlag, Bach-Archiv, Leipzig); miniature scores by Dürr (Bä), Grischkat (Eul); score by Max Schneider (B&H); vocal scores by Edgar and Ivor Atkins (Nov), Whittaker (OUP) Schneider (B&H), Stanford (Stainer & Bell), Lanon (Ricordi), W Sterndale-Bennett (Nov).

St Mark Passion (247) score and choral score by Hellmann (Hänssler/Nov).

St Luke Passion (246) vocal score by Radeke (B&H).

St John Passion (245) miniature score by Schering (Eul); score by Kretschmer (Peters); vocal scores by Arthur Mendel

(Schirmer), by Ivor Atkins (Nov), by F Rösler (Peters) Günther Raphael (B&H) Lanon (Ricordi).

Christmas Oratorio (248) facsimile of the autograph (Bä); miniature scores by Walter Blankenburg and Dürr (Bä), Schering (Eul); vocal scores by Raphael (B&H), with English translation by Troutbeck (Nov), by Lanon (Ricordi).

Easter Oratorio (249) score by Smend (Bä), score and choral score by Hellmann (Hänssler/Nov); vocal scores by Raphael (B&H), by Edgar Hunt with English translation by Carol Grey (Schott), sinfonia 1 and 3 by Whittaker (OUP).

Sanctus no 2 D major (238) vocal score by Paul Steinitz (OUP), by David Pinkman with English translation by Jean Lunn (Peters, New York).

Sanctus no 4 G major (240) vocal score by Walter Ehret (Boosey & Hawkes, New York).

Sanctus no 5 D major (241) score and choral score by Harrassowitz (Hänssler/Nov).

MOTETS

Fürchte dich nicht, ich bin bei dir (228) scores by Neumann with English translations by W E Buszin (Peters), Whittaker (OUP), Ameln and Walters (Möseler/Nov).

Der Geist hilft unsrer Schwachheit auf (226) facsimile of the autograph (Bä); scores by Neumann with English translation by Buszin (Peters), by Ameln and Walters (Möseler/Nov), by West with English translation by W Bartholomew (Nov).

Jesu mein Freude (227) scores by Neumann with English translation by Buszin (Peters), by Whittaker (OUP), by Ameln and Walters (Möseler/Nov).

Komm, Jesu, komm (229) scores by Neumann with English translation by Buszin (Peters), by Ameln and Walters (Möseler/Nov).

Lobet den Herrn, alle Heiden (230) scores by Neumann with English translation by Buszin (Peters), by Ameln and Walters (Möseler/Nov).

O Jesu Christ, mein's Lebens Licht (118) see under cantatas (no 118).

Singet dem Herrn ein neues Lied (225) facsimile of the autograph (Bä); miniature score by Fritz Stein (Eul); vocal scores
by West with English translation by W Bartholomew (Nov), by
Scott with English translation by B E Bulman (OUP), by Neumann with English translation by Buszin (Peters), by Ameln and
and Walters (Möseler/Nov).

CHORALES

Four Part Chorales (253-458) by Ludwig Erk revised by
Friedrich Smend (Peters), by Woldemar Bargiel (Bote & Bock,
Berlin), by Fritz Lubrich (Schweere & Haake, Bremen), by
Smend (Bä), by Terry with historical introduction, notes and
critical appendices (OUP), miniature score (LPS).

SONGS AND ARIAS

*Songs and arias complete including songs from Anna Mag-
dalena Notebook (439-523)* by E Naumann (B&H), also for
low voice by F Martin (B&H), for four part choir by Franz
Wüllner (B&H), miniature score (LPS).

Geistliche Lieder aus Schemellis Gesangbuch (439-507) by
Max Seiffert (Bä).

HYMNS

Original hymn tunes for congregational use by Terry (OUP).

PSALM

The 51st "Tilge, Höchster, meine Sünde" (arrangement from
Pergolesi's 'Stabat Mater') score and choral score by Hellmann
(Hänssler/Nov).

Instrumental music   ORGAN

Complete works and large collections: The first complete,
critically edited collection was that by F C Griepenkerl and
Ferdinand Roitsch, which appeared in 1844-50 in 8 vols (Peters)
later expanded to 9. Vol 9 was re-edited first by Karl Straube
and later by Hermann Keller. A similarly comprehensive edition
by Ernst Naumann in 9 vols (B&H) is being issued in a revised
edition by Heinz Lohmann.

The standard nineteenth century English edition was made by W T Best, the famous organist of St George's Hall, Liverpool, and revised by A Eaglefield Hull (Augener). More scholarly was that by Sir J F Bridge, James Higgs, J E West and Sir Ivor Atkins (20 books in 5 vols, Novello). But when it too became outdated by the advance of scholarship, Walter Emery undertook a revision, of which only vol 4 (1-3 of the 6 trio sonatas), vol 8 (miscellaneous) and vol 15 (Orgelbüchlein) appeared. Subsequently another revised edition of the 20 vol collection (Novello) was begun by Emery and Sir John Dykes-Bower, but again only three volumes appeared: vols 1 (eight short preludes and fugues), 4 and 5 (nos 1-3 and 4-6 respectively of the six trio sonatas).

A notable French edition was that by the famous organist Marcel Dupré (12 vols, Bornemann, Paris). The most comprehensive American edition is that in 8 vols by Charles Widor, Albert Schweitzer and Edouard Nies-Berger (Schirmer, New York); each volume has 'observations on the manner of performing the preludes and fugues, and suggestions for the interpretations of the compositions'.

Reprints of the nineteenth century Bach-Gesellschaft collected edition (B&H) are available in miniature score (Kalmus and also Lea Pocket Scores).

Smaller collections: Peters issue an edition of the chorale preludes in 3 vols comprising the Orgelbüchlein, the Clavierübung part 3, 6 chorales and 18 chorales. There is a two-vol edition of the organ chorales by Hans Luedke (B&H); they are also edited for manuals only by Hermann Keller (Bä). Ten are available in a piano transcription by Busoni (B&H). A Dover Press reprint in one vol from three vols of the Bach-Gesellschaft edition contains all the items in the three-vol Peters edition plus the six trio sonatas.

Single works and groups: In order to provide a link between the items listed here and in the discography in the next chapter, the works for organ, like the cantatas, are listed in the order of the thematic catalogue by Schmieder.

525-530 Six trio sonatas by Gotthold Frotscher (Mitteldeutscher Verlag, Halle); for two pianos by Victor Babin (Boosey & Hawkes).

531-552 Preludes and fugues 18 preludes and fugues (531-548), selections for piano by Carl Tausig (Augener), and by Eugen d'Albert (Forberg, Leipzig). 532 in D major for piano by Reger (Augener), Busoni (B&H), Johana and Roy Harris (Mills Music, New York); for orchestra by Respighi (Ricordi). 535 in G minor for piano by Michael Zadora (Schirmer, New York). 537 in C minor for orchestra by Elgar (Nov). 538 in D minor for piano by Joseph Prostakoff (Schirmer, New York); for two pianos by Vera Towsey (OUP) and Sir W H Harris (Novello). 540 in F major for piano by Gabriel Pierné (Leduc, Paris) and Joseph Röntgen (B&H); for two pianos by Vivian Langrish (OUP); for three pianos by Percy Grainger (Schirmer, New York). 541 in G major for piano duet by Gerrard Williams (OUP); for two pianos by John Odom (Curwen). 542 in G minor for piano by Liszt edited by Edwin Hughes (Schirmer, New York); for two pianos by C H Stuart Duncan (Ashdown). 543-548 for piano by Liszt, edited by Emil von Sauer (Peters). 543 in A minor for piano by Liszt (Augener), by Liszt edited by Edwin Hughes (Schirmer, New York); by Liszt arranged for piano duet by Ernest Haywood (OUP). 544 in B minor, facsimile of the autograph by O E Deutsch (Heffer, Cambridge) and Georg Kinsky (UE). 545 in C major, a version in Bb by Walter Emery with additional movements from other Bach works (Nov). 546 in C minor for two pianos by Robin Miller (Nov). 552 in E flat major (from Clavierübung III); for piano by Reger (Augener), prelude only by Leonard Borwick (Augener); for orchestra by Schoenberg (UE).

553-560 8 Little preludes and fugues by Caspar Koch with Hammond organ registration by Porter Heaps (Volkswein, Pittsburgh), by Alec Rowley (Joseph Williams), by Karl Straube (Peters); for piano by Frederick C Schreiber (Schirmer, NY).

564-6 Toccatas by Henry Coleman (Leonard, Gould & Boltler). 564 in C major for piano by Busoni (B&H); for military band by Denis Plater (Boosey). 565 in D minor for piano by Reger (Augener), Busoni (B&H); simplified arrangement for piano by Granville Bantock (Paxton); for two pianos by York Bowen (Elkin), C H Stuart Duncan (Lengnick), Mario Bragiotti

(Schirmer, New York); for orchestra by Sir Henry Wood (OUP); for military band by Denis Wright (Chappell); for piano and strings by Herbert Horrocks (OUP).

576 Fugue in G major for piano by Leonard Borwick (Augener).

578 Fugue in G minor for piano by Leonard Borwick (Augener), by N D de Knesz (OUP), by Olga Samaroff (Elkan Vogel, Philadelphia); for two pianos by Catherine Kramer (Pro-Art Publications, New York), by Christopher à Becket Williams (Peters), by C H Stuart Duncan (Ashdown); for orchestra by Lucien Cailliet (Carl Fischer, New York).

582 Passacaglia in C minor by Sandra della Libera (Zanibon, Padua); for piano by Eugen d'Albert (Bote & Bock, Berlin); for two pianos by Abram Chasins (J Fischer, New York); for orchestra by Respighi (Ricordi).

590 Pastorale in F major by Günther Ramin (Bä); for piano by W G Whittaker (OUP), by Dinu Lipatti (Schott); for small orchestra by Vittorio Gui (UE).

595 Concerto in C major (arranged by Bach from a violin concerto by Johann Ernst, Duke of Weimar) for two pianos by Robin Miller (Ashdown).

599-644 Orgelbüchlein 11 choral preludes for two pianos by C H Stuart Duncan (Schirmer, New York); 22 choral preludes for recorders by John Beckett (Schott). 622 'O Mensch, bewein dein Sünde gross' for string orchestra by Reger (Augener). 631 'Komm, Gott' for orchestra by Schoenberg (UE).

645-51 6 Chorales (Schübler) no 1 (645) 'Wachet auf' by H G Ley (Year Book Press), by H K Andrews (OUP); for piano by Harriet Cohen (OUP), by Myra Hess (OUP), by Leonard Borwick (Augener); for piano duet by Cohen (OUP); for cello and piano by William Alwyn (OUP).

651-68 18 Chorales no 1 (651) fantasia super 'Komm Heiliger Geist' facsimile of the autograph by Peter Wackernagel (Merseburger, Leipzig).

669-89 Chorale preludes from Clavierübung III (St Anne or Trinity prelude and fugue is entered under preludes and fugues at 552) 6 preludes (672, 673, 671, 675, 683, 687) re-arranged for organ by Stainton de B Taylor (Peters). 681 fughetta super 'Wir glauben all' an einen Gott' for string orchestra by Vaughan Williams and Arnold Foster (OUP); for symphony orchestra by Fabien Sevitzky (Birchard, Boston).

714-740 *Miscellaneous chorale preludes.* 721 'Erbarm dich' for piano by Leonard Borwick (OUP). 727 'Herzlich tut mich verlangen' for orchestra by Lucien Cailliet (Elkan-Vogel, Philadelphia). 734 'Nun freut euch, lieben Christen, g'mein' for piano by Borwick (Augener).

769 *Canonic variations on 'Von Himmel hoch'* by Friedrich Smend (Bä and B&H); for orchestra by Roger Vuataz (Ars Viva, Vienna); for chorus and orchestra by Stravinsky, score and min score (Boosey & Hawkes).

CLAVIER

Complete works by Hans Bischoff (7 vols, Steingräber, Wiesbaden), by Czerny and others (23 vols, Peters), by Busoni, Egon Petri and Bruno Mugellini (B&H), also in miniature score (LPS and Kalmus).

Smaller collections. Two capriccios, aria variata, fantasies, fugues and 'Vorstudien' to the 'Forty-eight' by Herman Keller (Peters). Sonatas and sonata movements by Keller (Peters). The Chromatic fantasy and fugue, the Italian concerto, the Fantasy in C minor, the Prelude and fugue in C minor by Hans von Bülow and Max Vogrich (Schirmer, New York). Smaller pieces by Alexander Siloti (B&H). Twenty-four little preludes and fugues (895, 899, 900, 924-930, 932-939, 941, 942,951-953, 961) by Keller (Peters). *Introduction to the performance of Bach: a progressive anthology* by Rosalind Tureck (3 books, OUP). Easier piano pieces by H J Schulze (Peters).

Aria variata alla maniera italiana (989) by F A Roitzsch (Peters), by H Bischoff (Peters).

Capriccio in B-dur sopra la lontananza del suo fratello diletissimo (992) by Hermann Roth (Drei Masken Verlag, Munich), by James Friskin (J Fischer, New York), by Stainton de B Taylor (Peters).

Chromatic fantasy and fugue (903) by C Reinecke (B&H), by Heinrich Schenker revised by Oswald Jonas (UE), by von Bülow

(Ashdown), by Emil von Sauer (Peters), by Edwin Fischer (Hansen, Copenhagen); for cello and piano by Busoni (B&H); the fantasy only by Liszt (Haslinger), and for viola solo by Kodaly (Boosey & Hawkes).

Clavierbüchlein vor Wilhelm Friedemann Bach facsimile of the autograph by Ralph Kirkpatrick (Yale University Press); by Keller (Peters); selection of easy pieces by Helma Trede (Schott); little preludes and fugues, after the Clavierbüchlein vor W F Bach and copies from the circle of Bach's pupils by Rudolf Steglich (Henle, Munich).

Clavierbüchlein für Anna Magdalena Bach see p100 *Noten-büchlein*.

Clavierübung all four parts (part 3 comprising only the four duets) by Kurt Soldan (Peters). Part 1, *The six partitas* by Czerny, Griepenkehrl and Roitzsch (Peters), Rudolf Steglich (Henle, Munich); nos 1-3 by Petri (B&H). Part 2 *Italian concerto* (971) by von Bülow (Ashdown), by Griepenkehrl (Peters); for two pianos by Harold Bauer (Schirmer, New York). Part 2 *Overture in French style (831)* by Petri (B&H), the original version in C minor by Hans David (Schott); the Echo freely arranged for Organ by Karg-Elert (Carl Simon, Berlin). Part 3 *Four duets* (802-5) by Busoni (B&H); for violin and viola by Walther Davisson (B&H); for violin and cello by Paul Grümmer (Litolff). Part 3 *Organ works* see under organ 552 and 669-689. Part 4 *Goldberg variations (988)* by Petri (B&H), by Kirkpatrick (Schirmer, New York); for two pianos by Joseph Rheinberger (Kistner, Leipzig), Max Reger (Kistner, Lippstadt); for organ by Wilhelm Middelschulte (Kahnt, Leipzig).

Concertos (972-987) arranged by Bach from works by Vivaldi, Marcello, Telemann and others, by Reinecke (B&H), by Mugellini (B&H); for piano solo by Arnold Schering (Peters). 974 in D minor from Alessandro Marcello's oboe concerto by Adolf Hoffmann (Möseler, Wolfenbüttel).

English suites see p101 *Suites*.

Fantasias and fugues. 904 in A minor by Reinecke (B&H), by Busoni (B&H), by von Bülow (Ricordi); for organ by Harry Wall (Leonard, Gould & Boltler); the fugue only for string orchestra by Arnold Foster (OUP). 905 in D minor by Busoni as 'Sonatina brevis in signo Joannis Sebastiani Magni' (B&H).

906 in C minor by Busoni (B&H) including completion of the fugue and Bach's clavier arrangement (968) of the adagio from Sonata for solo violin (1005); fantasia only by Reinecke (B&H), by Czerny (Peters), by Edwin Fischer (Ullstein), by Betty Reeves (Walsh Holmes); 907 in B flat major and 908 in D major by Czerny (Peters).

French suites see p101 *Suites*.

Fughetta in C minor (961) by Reinecke (B&H), by Busoni (B&H), by Czerny (Peters), by Reger and Schmid-Lindner (Schott).

Fugues 944 in A minor by Czerny (Peters). 945-951 by Reinecke (B&H). 947 in A minor for strings by Ralph Nicholson (OUP). 952; 953, both in C major, by Reinecke (B&H), by Czerny (Peters), by Reger and Schmid-Linder (Schott). 954 & 955 both in B flat major by Reinecke (B&H). 956-9 by Petri (B&H).

Goldberg variations (988) see above p99 *Clavierübung* part 4.

Inventions (772-801), ie Two part inventions (772-786) and Three part inventions or sinfonien (787-801). Facsimile of the entire autograph by Kirkpatrick (Yale University Press). Two and Three part inventions by Ludwig Landshoff (Peters), by William Mason (Schirmer, New York), by James Friskin (J Fischer, Glen Rock), by Bischoff (Schirmer, New York), by Rudolf Steglich (Henle, Munich), by Arthur Alexander (Associated Board of the Royal Schools of Music), by Reinecke (B&H), by Busoni (B&H), by Czerny (Peters). Two part inventions for piano duet by L V Saar with his second piano part (Schirmer, New York); for violin and viola by Ferdinand David (B&H); no 8 (779) for orchestra by Cyril Scott (Elkin).

Italian concerto (971) see above p99 *Clavierübung* part 2.

Notenbüchlein für Anna Magdalena Bach by Arnold Schering revised by Werner Breikoff (Hofmeister, Frankfurt), by Georg von Dadelsen (Bä). Selections by Bartók (Zenemukiado Vállalat, Budapest), by Franz Ludwig (Schott), by Emil von Sauer (Peters).

Instrumental music

Partitas see above p99 *Clavierübung* part 1.
Praeambula see above p100 *Inventions*.
Preludes and fugues see below *Well-tempered clavier*.
Suites. English suites (806-811) after Czerny but no editor (Schirmer, New York), by Petri (B&H), by Edwin Fischer (Hansen, Copenhagen), by Alessandro Longo (Ricordi), by Rudolf Steglich (Henle, Munich), by Alfred Kreutz (Peters). French suites (812-817) by Orlando Morgan (Ashdown), by Busoni revised by Petri (B&H), by Steglich (Henle, Munich); movements from nos 1, 3, 5 and 6 as 'An orchestral suite' by Honegger (UE). Suites 820, 821, 823, 824 by Petri (B&H).

Toccatas (910-916) by Edwin Hughes (Schirmer, New York), by Hermann Keller (Peters), by Steglich (Henle, Munich), by Reinecke (B&H); 910-913 by Petri (B&H); 914-916 by Busoni (B&H).

Well-tempered clavier (846-893), *ie* Das wohltemperiertes Klavier or 48 Preludes and fugues. Facsimile of the autograph of part 1 (Deutscher Verlag für Musik, Leipzig). Parts 1 and 2, probably the most frequently edited of all Bach's works, by Busoni (B&H), by Mugellini (B&H), by Czerny (Peters, and Augener), by Adolf Ruthardt (Peters), by Eugen d'Albert (Cotta, Stuttgart), by Fauré (Durand), by Harold Brooke (Novello), by Alfredo Casella (Curci, Milan), by Sir Donald Tovey (Associated Board of the Royal Schools of Music), by Bartók (Rozsavolgyi, Budapest), by Franz Kroll (Peters), by Otto von Irmer (Henle, Munich), by Hans Bischoff (Schirmer, New York), by Alfred Kreutz (part 1) and Hermann Keller (part 2) (Peters), by Edwin Hughes (Schirmer, New York); for piano by Glen Gould (Music Sales). Of the older editions Bischoff's, which Schirmer reprinted from the Steingräber plates, is probably the best. The generally accepted English edition is Tovey's, although its editorial principles are now rather outmoded. The best of the recent continental editions is Irmer's.

LUTE

Complete works by Hans Dagobert Bruger (Julius Zwissler, Wolfenbüttel). *Suite in E minor (996)* for guitar by Julian Bream (Faber); for piano by Petri (B&H).

Partita in C minor (997) for keyboard by Howard Ferguson (Schott), by Petri (B&H).

Prelude, fugue and allegro in E flat major (998) for piano by Reinecke (B&H), by Busoni (B&H), by Bischoff (Peters).

Prelude in C minor (999) for piano by Reinecke (B&H), by Busoni (B&H), by Czerny (Peters), by Reger and Schmid-Lindner (Schott); for viola and piano by Kodály (Boosey & Hawkes).

CHAMBER MUSIC

Flute solo. Sonata in A minor (1013) by Maximilian Schwedler with piano accompaniment written by G Schreck ad libitum (Peters), by H P Schmitz (Bä), by René Le Roy (Durand, Paris); miniature score (LPS).

Flute and clavier. Six sonatas (1030-1035) by Louis Fleury (Durand, Paris), by Louis Moyse with 1013 and Sonata in G minor 1020 (Schirmer, New York), by Jules Mouquet (Lemoine, Paris), by Ferdinand David (Peters), by Schreck and Schwedler (Peters), by Barge, Spiro and Todt (B&H); miniature score with three sonatas for viola da gamba and clavier (LPS). Three sonatas (1030-2) by Kurt Soldan (Peters), by Henry Geehl, flute part by Charles Stainer (B&H). Sonata in B minor (1030) facsimile of the autograph (Deutscher Verlag für Musik, Leipzig).

Violin solo. Three sonatas (1001, 1003. 1005) and three partitas (1002, 1004, 1006) facsimile of the autograph by Günter Hausswald (Bä); edited by Jean Champeil (Heugel, Paris), by Leopold Auer (Carl Fischer, New York,) by Jan Hambourg (OUP), by D C Dounis (Strad Edition), by Carl Flesch (Peters, New York), by Maxim Jacobsen (Peters), by Eduard Hermann (Schirmer, New York), by Joseph Hellmesberger revised by Carl Hermann (Nov), by Walther Davisson (B&H); miniature score with cello suites (LPS); with piano accompaniment arranged by Schumann (B&H). Partita no 2 (1004) the chaconne for viola by Lionel Tertis (Augener); for violin with piano accompaniment by Mendelssohn (B&H); for piano (left hand) by Brahms; for piano by Busoni (B&H); after Busoni for orchestra by Maximilian Steinberg (Edition Russe de Musique); for orchestra by Casella (Carisch, Milan). Partita no 3 (1006) for piano and violin by Kreisler (Schott); for piano by Rachmaninov (C Foley, New York). Three sonatas (1001, 1003, 1005) with three of the cello suites freely adapted and transcribed for piano solo by Leopold Godowsky (Carl Fischer, New York).

Violin and clavier. Six sonatas (1014-1019) by Ferdinand David (Peters), by Hans Eppstein (Henle, Munich), by Ernst Neumann (B&H), by Rudolf Gerber (Peters), by Hugo Kortschak and Edwin Hughes (Schirmer, New York), by Debussy (Durand, Paris), by Maxim Jacobsen (Peters); miniature score (LPS). Sonata in G major (1021) by Adolf Busch and Friedrich Blume (publication of the Neue Bach Gesellschaft Jahrgang XXX Heft 1). Sonata in F major (1022) by Ludwig Landshoff (Peters). Sonata in E minor (1023) by Walther Davisson (B&H), by Howard Ferguson (Schott). Fugue in G minor (1026) by Ferguson (OUP).

Cello solo. Six suites (1007-12) by Julius Klengel (B&H), by Paul Tortelier (Galliard, Galaxy, New York), by Paul Grümmer and E H Müller von Asow (Doblinger), by Fritz Gaillard (Schirmer, New York), by Enrico Mainardi (Schott), by August Wenzinger (Bä), by M R and Lieff Rosanoff (Galaxy, New York); miniature score with six solo violin partitas and sonatas (LPS); for viola by Louis Svečenski (Schirmer, New York), by Watson Forbes (OUP); for clarinet by Ulysse Delécluse (Leduc, Paris); 1008, 1009, 1011 only, with the three violin sonatas, freely adapted and transcribed for piano solo by Leopold Godowsky (Carl Fischer, New York).

Viola da gamba, or cello, and clavier. Three sonatas (1027-9) by Julius Klengel (B&H), by Rolf von Leyden (Peters), by Debussy and Pierre Fournier (Durand, Paris); for viola and piano by Ernst Neumann (B&H).

Two violins and bass. Sonata in C major (1037) by Christian Döbereiner (Schott), by Claude Crussard (Foetisch, Lausanne).

Flute, violin and clavier. Sonata in G major (1038) by Ludwig Landshoff (Peters).

Two flutes and clavier. Sonata in G major (1034) by Landshoff (Peters).

ORCHESTRAL

Concertos. Violin in A minor (1041), E major (1042), D minor (1043) all miniature scores by Arnold Schering (Eul), no editor (LPS, also Boosey & Hawkes), by S W Dehn (Peters). 1041 and 1042 no editor (Ricordi); for violin and piano by Walther Davisson (B&H), by Carl Flesch (Zenemukiado Vallalat, Budapest). 1041 for violin and piano by David Oistrakh (Peters). 1042 for violin and piano by A Siloti (Carl Fischer, New York), by Max Strub (Peters). 1043 for two pianos and piano by Eduard Hermann (Boosey & Hawkes), with the second violin part for viola by Lionel Tertis (Boosey & Hawkes). Flute, violin and clavier in A minor (1044) by Schering (Eul), by Dehn and Roitzsch (Peters); score, no editor, and parts by Reger (B&H). The 'Brandenburg Concertos' (1046-1051) facsimile of the autograph by Peter Wackernagel (Peters); all six concertos by August Wenzinger (Bä) (the best modern edition), miniature scores from the Neue Bach Ausgabe; miniature scores also by Schering (Eul), no editor (Boosey & Hawkes, also Ricordi and LPS), by Kurt Soldan (Peters), by Mandyczewski, Gal, Orel and Geiringer (Wiener Phiharmonischer Verlag); for two pianos by Reger (Peters). 1046-1050 with an introduction by Gordon Jacob (Penguin Books). 1049 no 4 by Sir Henry Wood (Boosey & Hawkes). 1051 no 6 for two violas and piano by Watson Forbes (Peters).

Concertos—arrangements. Miniature scores (LPS). Clavier in D minor (1052) miniature scores by Arnold Schering (Eul), no editor (Boosey & Hawkes); for two pianos by Edwin Hughes (Schirmer, New York), by Adolf Ruthardt (Augener; Peters, New York); free arrangement by Busoni (B&H); reconstructed for violin and piano with violin part by Szigeti (Boosey & Hawkes). Concerto for oboe in E major (from 1053 and cantatas 169 and 49) by Hermann Töttcher and Gottfried Müller (Sikorski, Hamburg). Concertos in E major (1053) and A major (1055) score and parts by K Soldan (Peters). Concerto in F minor (1056) miniature score by Schering (Eul); for two pianos by Robert Teichmüller (Peters); in G minor for violin and piano by Ferdinand David (Augener); for violin and orchestra by

104

J B Jackson revised by W G Whittaker (OUP); also in G minor for oboe and strings by Winifred Radeke (B&H); the largo in numerous arrangements, *eg* for violin and piano by Szigeti (Carl Fischer, New York), for organ by S D Wolff (OUP), for piano by Harold Craxton (OUP). Violin concerto in D minor (1059 with material from cantata 35) reconstructed by Gottfried Frotscher; for violin and piano (Mitteldeutscher Verlag, Halle); for oboe and strings by Helmut Winschermann (Sikorski, Hamburg); also in E minor for flute and strings by Winifred Radeke (B&H); also in D minor for solo harpsichord or violin and orchestra completed by Werner Greitz (Möseler/Nov).

Concertos—clavier. Miniature scores (LPS). For two claviers in C minor (1060) and in C major (1061), miniature scores by Schering (Eul); for two pianos by Reger (B&H), by Adam Carse (Augener), by Harold Bauer (Schirmer, New York). 1060 in D minor for two violins and orchestra by Max Schneider (B&H). Concerto for three claviers in D minor (1063) and C major (1064) miniature scores by Schering (Eul); Concerto for three harpsichords (1064) by H Bauer (Schirmer, New York); in D major, for three violins by Rudolf Baumgartner (Hug, Zurich). Concerto for four claviers in A minor (1065) miniature score by Schering (Eul); score and parts by Roitzsch (Peters).

Overtures (Suites) 1-4 (1066-1069) miniature scores by Wilhelm Altmann (Eul), no editors (LPS, Boosey & Hawkes, Ricordi); score and parts by Reger (B&H), by Dehn (Peters), by Ludwig Landshoff (Peters). No 2 in B minor (1067) for flute and piano by Mátyás Seiber (Rudall, Carte).

An orchestral suite in four movements (from 1067, 1068) by Mahler, score and parts (Schirmer, New York).

Overture in G minor (1070, somewhat doubtful) by J N David (B&H).

MUSICAL OFFERING, THE ART OF FUGUE

Musical offering (1079) miniature scores, no editor (LPS, also Boosey & Hawkes); score by Landshoff (Peters); for string quartet, wind and clavier by Roger Vuataz (Ars Viva, Brussels), by H T David (Schirmer, New York); for orchestra by Ferdinand Oubradous (Oiseau Lyre, Monaco), by Igor Markevich (Boosey & Hawkes), by Hans Gál (Boosey & Hawkes), by Hermann Pillney (B&H). Three-part Ricercare for piano by Pillney (B&H). Canons, Fugues and Ricercari for organ by Gerhard Bunk (B&H). Trio sonata by Max Seiffert (B&H).

The Art of Fugue (1080) in original form by Wolfgang Gräser with piano version below (B&H); miniature scores by Hermann Diener (Bä), by Hans Gal (Boosey & Hawkes), no editor (LPS); for piano by Czerny (Peters), by Tovey (OUP); for piano duet by B G Seidlhofer (B&H); for organ by Helmut Walcha (Litolff/ Peters), by Heinz Lohmann (B&H), by E Power Biggs (H W Gray, New York); for string quartet by Roy Harris and M D H Norton (Schirmer, New York); in open score by Tovey and completed by him (OUP), by Gál (Boosey & Hawkes), by Albert Lunow (Peters); as a suite for chamber orchestra by Anthony Lewis (Boosey & Hawkes); for orchestra by Roger Vuataz (Ars Viva, Zurich).

CANONS

Fourteen canons (1087, newly discovered) for two organs or harpsichords, also for string trio and harpsichord or organ by Olivier Alain (Salabert, Paris); score by Christoph Wolff, preprint of Neue Bach Ausgabe (Bä).

Selected recordings of Bach's music

BY BRIAN REDFERN

The arrangement of the discography follows closely that used in the chapter on editions, with obvious omissions when no recording of a work is currently available. In order to avoid consultation of secondary lists and indexes I have tried to make the abbreviations of orchestral and other names self-explanatory. Performers are cited as appropriate in the order: soloists, choir, orchestra, conductor.

When the recording included in the list has been deleted, it may be possible to borrow it from one of the many public gramophone libraries which exist in both the United Kingdom and the United States. Quite often a recording reappears on a cheaper label after its deletion at a higher price.

Any second catalogue number given is American. If there is no second number, the recording may not be available in America except by import. American readers are referred to the excellent Schwann catalogue for prices and for a complete listing of American recordings, which include many only available in the United States, and which I have therefore not been able to hear. For British issues I have indicated the cheaper labels as follows: * medium price; † bargain.

CANTATAS

Complete edition: This is in progress of being issued by Telefunken with extensive notes in German, with translations in English and French. Each volume so far has contained two discs and the score of the nineteenth century Bach-Gesellschaft edition of the work. The performances are scholarly in the best sense. Male voices, including boys' voices, and authentic instruments are used. The standard so far has been very high. The performers include Esswood, Equiluz, Egmond, Wyatt, Nimsgern; Chorus Viennensis, King's College Chapel Choir, Vienna Boys' Choir; Vienna Concentus Musicus, Leonhardt Consort; Leonhardt, Harnoncourt.

1 Wie Schön leuchtet der Morgenstern, 2 Ach Gott, vom Himmel sieh' darein, 3 Ach Gott, wie manches Herzeleid, 4 Christ lag in Todesbanden
Complete edition vol 1. SKW 1; SKW 1.

5 Wo soll ich fliehen hin, 6 Bleib' bei uns, denn es will Abend werden, 7 Christ unser Herr zum Jordan kam, 8 Liebster Gott, wann werd ich sterben
Complete edition vol 2. SKW 2; SKW 2.

9 Es ist das Heil uns kommen her, 10 Meine Seel' erhebt den Herren, 11 Lobet Gott in seinen Reichen
Complete edition vol 3. SKW 3; SKW 3.

10 Meine Seel' erhebt den Herren
Ameling, Watts, Krenn, Rintzler; Vienna Academy Choir; Stuttgart Chamber Orch; Münchinger. *With* Magnificat. SXL 6400; London 26103.

12 Weinen, Klagen, Sorgen, Zagen, 13 Meine Seufzer, meine Tränen, 14 Wär' Gott nicht mit uns diese Zeit, 16 Herr Gott, dich loben wir
Complete edition vol 4. SKW 4; SKW 4.

17 Wer Dank opfert, der preiset mich, 18 Gleich wie der Regen, 19 Es erhub sich ein Streit, 20 O Ewigkeit, du Donnerwort
Complete edition vol 5. SKW 5; SKW 5.

21 Ich Hatte viel Bekümmernis, 22 Jesus nahm zu sich die Zwölfe, 23 Du wahrer Gott und Davids Sohn
Complete edition vol 6. SKW 6; SKW 6.

21 Ich hatte viel Bekümmernis
Burns, Márová, Melzer, Reich; Stuttgart Bach Society; Rilling.
* Supraphon 1120792.

*24 Ein ungefärbt Gemüte, 25 Es ist nichts Gesundes an
meinem Leibe, 26 Ach wie flüchtig, ach wie nichtig, 27 Wer
weiss, wie nahe mir mein Ende*
    Complete edition vol 7. SKW 7; SKW 7.
25 Es ist nichts Gesundes an meinem Leibe
    Wehrung, Gilvan, Messthaler; Stuttgart Motet Choir; Heidel-
berg Chamber Orch; Graulich. *With* Cantata 103 † BACH 1107.
27 Wer weiss, wie nahe mir mein Ende
    Hausmann, Watts, Equiluz, Egmond; Hamburg Monteverdi
Choir; Concerto Amsterdam; Schröder. *With* Cantatas 59, 118,
158. SAWT 9489; Telefunken S 9489.
*28 Gottlob! Nun geht das Jahr zu Ende, 29 Wir danken dir,
Gott, 30 Freue dich, erlöste Schar*
    Complete edition vol 8. SKW 8; SKW 8.
*31 Der Himmel lacht, 32 Liebster Jesu, mein Verlangen, 33
Allein zu dir, Herr Jesu Christ, 34 O ewiges Feuer, o Ursprung
der Liebe*
    Complete edition vol 9. SKW 9; SKW 9.
32 Liebster Jesu, mein Verlangen
    Ameling, Prey; Bach Soloists Choir & Orch; Winschermann.
With Cantata 57. 6500080; 6500080.
*35 Geist und Seele wird verwirret, 36 Schwingt freudig euch
empor, 37 Wer da glaubet und getauft wird, 38 Aus tiefer
Not schrei' ich zu dir*
    Complete edition vol 10. SKW 10; SKW 10.
*39 Brich dem Hungrigen dein Brot, 40 Dazu ist erschienen
der Sohn Gottes, 41 Jesu, nun sei gepreiset, 42 Am Abend
aber desselbigen Sabbats*
    Complete edition vol 11. SKW 11; SKW 11.
45 Es ist dir gesagt, Mensch, was gut ist
    Watts, Partridge, Krause; Suisse Romande & Lausanne Pro
Arte Choirs; Suisse Romande Orch; Ansermet. *With* Cantata
105. * SDD 384.
50 Nun ist das Heil und die Kraft
    Equiluz; Vienna Boys' Choir; Vienna Concentus Musicus;
Harnoncourt. *With* Cantatas 83, 197. *Not part of complete
series.* SAWT 9539; Telefunken S 9539.

51 *Jauchzet Gott in allen Lande*
   Ameling; German Bach Soloists; Winschermann. *With* Cantata 199. 6500014; 6500014.
   Giebel; Concerto Amsterdam; Schröder. *With* Cantata 202. SAWT 9513; Telefunken S 9513.
53 *Schlage doch, gewünschte Stunde*
   Watts, Philomusica of London; Dart. *With* Cantatas 54, 200.
   * SOL 60003; Oiseau Lyre 60003.
54 *Widerstehe doch der Sünde*
   Watts; Philomusica of London; Dart. *With* Cantatas 53, 200.
   * SOL 60003; Oiseau Lyre 60003.
55 *Ich armer Mensch, ich Sündenknecht*
   Gilvan; Mannheim Bach Choir; Heidelberg Chamber Orch; Göttsche. *With* Cantatas 160, 189. † BACH 1119.
56 *Ich will den Kreuzstab gerne tragen*
   Shirley-Quirk; St Anthony Singers; Academy of St Martin in the Fields; Marriner. *With* Cantata 82. * SOL 280; Oiseau Lyre S 280.
   Souzay; Berlin Capella; German Bach Soloists; Winschermann. *With* Cantata 82. SAL 3767.
57 *Selig ist der Mann*
   Ameling, Prey; Bach Soloists Choir & Orch; Winschermann. *With* Cantata 32. 6500080; 6500080.
59 *Wer mich liebet*
   Hausmann, Egmond; Hamburg Monteverdi Choir; Concerto Amsterdam; Schröder. *With* Cantatas 27, 118, 158. SAWT 9489; Telefunken S 9489.
61 *Nun komm, der Heiden Heiland*
   Reichelt, Altmeyer, Wollitz; Barmen-Germarke Choir; German Bach Soloists; Kahlhöfer. *With* Cantata 132. † BACH 1117.
67 *Halt im Gedächtnis Jesum Christ*
   Watts, Krenn, Krause; Lausanne Pro Arte Chorus; Suisse Romande Orch; Ansermet. *With* Cantatas 101, 130. SXL 6392; London 26098.
74 *Wer mich liebet, der wird mein Wort halten*
   Cotrubas, Hamari, Equiluz, Reimer; Netherlands Vocal

Vocal music

Ensemble; German Bach Soloists; Winschermann. *With* Cantata 147. 65000386.

80 Ein feste Burg ist unser Gott
 Giebel, Töpper, Schreier, Adam; St Thomas's Church Choir; Leipzig Gewandhaus Orch Soloists; Mauersberger. *With* Cantata 140. 198407; ARC 198407.
 Ameling, Baker, Altmeyer, Sotin; South German Madrigal Choir; Consortium Musicum; Gönnenwein. *With* Cantata 140. ASD 2381.

82 Ich habe genug
 Shirley-Quirk; St Anthony Singers; Academy of St Martin in the Field; Marriner. *With* Cantata 56. * SOL 280; Oiseau Lyre S 280.
 Souzay; Berlin Capella. German Bach Soloists; Winschermann. *With* Cantata 56. SAL 3767.
 Baker; Ambrosian Singers; Bath Festival Orch; Menuhin. *With* Cantata 169. ASD 2302; Angel S 36419.

83 Erfreute Zeit im neuen Bunde
 Equiluz, Egmond; Vienna Boys' Choir; Vienna Concentus Musicus; Harnoncourt. *With* Cantatas 50, 197. *Not part of complete series.* SAWT 9539; Telefunken S 9539.

89 Was soll ich aus dir machen, Ephraim
 Armstrong, Watts, Egmond; Hamburg Monteverdi Chorus; Concerto Amsterdam; Schröder. *With* Cantatas 90, 161. SAWT 9540; Telefunken S 9540.

90 Es reifet euch ein schrecklich Ende
 Watts, Equiluz, Egmond; Hamburg Monteverdi Chorus; Concerto Amsterdam; Schröder. *With* Cantatas 89, 161. SAWT 9540; Telefunken S 9540.

101 Nimm von uns Herr, du treuer Gott
 Ameling, Watts, Krenn, Krause; Lausanne Pro Arte Chorus; Suisse Romande Orch; Ansermet. *With* Cantatas 67, 130. SXL 6392; London 26098.

103 Ihr werdet weinen und heulen
 Waldbauer, Gilvan; Stuttgart Motet Choir; Heidelberg Chamber Orchestra; Graulich. *With* Cantata 25. † BACH 1107.

105 Herr, gehe nicht ins Gericht
Giebel, Watts, Partridge, Krause; Suisse Romande & Lausanne Pro Arte Choirs; Suisse Romande Orch; Ansermet. *With* Cantata 45. * SDD 384.

106 Gottes Zeit ist die allerbeste Zeit
Falk, Villisech; Hamburg Monteverdi Choir; Leonhardt Consort; Jürgens. *With* Cantata 182. SAWT 9443; Telefunken S 9443.

118 O Jesu Christ, mein's Lebens Licht
Hamburg Monteverdi Choir; Concerto Amsterdam; Schröder. *With* Cantatas 27, 59, 158. SAWT 9489; Telefunken S 9489.

130 Herr Gott, dich loben alle wir
Ameling, Watts, Krenn, Krause; Lausanne Pro Arte Chorus; Suisse Romande Orch; Ansermet. *With* Cantatas 67, 101. SXL 6392; London 26098.

131 Aus der Tiefe rufe ich, Herr, zu dir
Jenkins, Noble; London Bach Society Chorus; Steinitz Bach Players; Steinitz. *With* Handel. Wedding anthem, 'Sing unto God'. * CSD 3741; Nonesuch 71294.

132 Bereitet die Wege, bereitet die Bahn
Reichelt, Rutgers, Altmeyer, Wollitz; German Bach Soloists; Kahlhöfer. *With* Cantata 61. † BACH 1117.

140 Wachet auf, ruft uns die Stimme
Giebel, Schreier, Adam; St Thomas's Church Choir; Leipzig Gewandhaus Orch Soloists; Mauersberger. *With* Cantata 80. 198407; ARC 198407.

Ameling, Altmeyer, Sotin; South German Madrigal Choir; Consortium Musicum; Gönnenwein. *With* Cantata 80. ASD 2381.

147 Herz und Mund und Tat und Leben
Cotrubas, Hamari, Equiluz, Reimer; Netherlands Vocal Ensemble; German Bach Soloists; Winschermann. *With* Cantata 74. 6500386.

Ameling, Baker, Partridge, Shirley-Quirk; King's College Cambridge Choir; Academy of St Martin in the Fields; Willcocks. *With* Motets 2, 4, 6. * HQS 1254; Angel S 36804.

158 Der Friede sei mit dir
Egmond; Hamburg Monteverdi Choir; Concerto Amsterdam;
Schröder. *With* Cantatas 27, 59, 118. SAWT 9489; Telefunken S 9489.
159 Sehet, wir geh'n hinauf gen Jerusalem.
Baker, Tear, Shirley-Quirk; St Anthony Singers; Academy
of St Martin in the Fields; Marriner. *With* Cantata 170. * SOL
295; Oiseau Lyre S 295.
160 Ich weiss, dass mein Erlöser lebt
Gilvan; Heidelberg Chamber Orch; Göttsche. *With* Cantatas
55, 189. † BACH 1119.
161 Komm, du süsse Todesstunde
Watts, Equiluz; Hamburg Monteverdi Chorus; Concerto
Amsterdam; Schröder. *With* Cantatas 89, 90. SAWT 9540;
Telefunken S 9540.
169 Gott soll allein mein Herze haben
Baker; Ambrosian Singers; Bath Festival Orch; Menuhin.
With Cantata 82. ASD 2302; Angel S 36419.
170 Vergnügte Ruh', beliebte Seelenlust
Baker; Academy of St Martin in the Fields; Marriner. *With*
Cantata 159. * SOL 295; Oiseau Lyre S 295.
172 Erschallet, ihr Lieder
Wehrung, Waldbauer, Gilvan, Achenbach; Tübing Cantata
Choir; South German Youth Symphony Orch; Achenbach.
With Cantata 192. † BACH 1111.
182 Himmelskönig, sei willkommen
Falk, Hoff, Villisech, Hamburg Monteverdi Choir; Leonhardt
Consort; Jürgens. *With* Cantata 106. SAWT 9443; Telefunken
S 9443.
189 Meine Seele rühmt und preist
Gilvan; Heidelberg Chamber Orch; Göttsche. *With* Cantatas
55, 160. † BACH 1119.
192 Nun danket alle Gott
Wehrung, Achenbach; Tübing Cantata Choir; South German
Youth Symphony Orch; Achenbach. *With* Cantata 172.
† BACH 1111.

197 Gott ist unsre Zuversicht
Equiluz, Egmond; Vienna Boys' Choir; Vienna Concentus Musicus; Harnoncourt. *With* Cantatas 50, 83. *Not part of complete series.* SAWT 9539; Telefunken S 9539.

198 Lass, Fürstin, lass noch einen Strahl
Hausmann, Watts, Equiluz, Egmond; Hamburg Monteverdi Choir; Concerto Amsterdam; Jürgens. SAWT 9496; Telefunken S 9496.

199 Mein Herze Schwimmt im Blut
Ameling; German Bach Soloists; Winschermann. *With* Cantata 51. 6500014; Phillips 6500014.

200 Bekennen will ich seinen Namen
Watts; Philomusica of London; Dart. *With* Cantatas 53, 54.
* SOL 60003; Oiseau Lyre 60003.

202 Weichet nur, betrübte Schatten
Giebel; Concerto Amsterdam; Schröder. *With* Cantata 51. SAWT 9513; Telefunken S 9513.
Ameling; Academy of St Martin in the Fields; Marriner. *With* Cantata 209. ASD 2876.
Buckel; Württemberg Chamber Orch; Ewerhart. *With* Cantata 212. † TV 34042S; Turnabout 34042.

203 Amore traditore
Villisech; Leonhardt Consort. *With* Cantata 209. SAWT 9465; Telefunken S 9465.
Ocker; Württemberg Chamber Orch; Ewerhart. *With* Cantata 211. † TV 34071S; Turnabout 34071.

204 Ich bin in mir vergnügt
Speiser; Württemberg Chamber Orch; Ewerhart. *With* Cantata 209. † TV 34127S; Turnabout 34127.

206 Schleicht, spielende Wellen
Jacobeit, Matthès, Brand, Villisech; Hamburg Monteverdi Choir; Amsterdam Chamber Orch; Rieu. SAWT 9425; Telefunken S 9425.

208 Was mir behagt
Spoorenberg, Jacobeit, Brand, Villisech; Hamburg Monteverdi Choir; Amsterdam Chamber Orch; Rieu. SAWT 9427.

Vocal music

209 Non sa che sia dolore
Ameling; Academy of St Martin in the Fields; Marriner.
With Cantata 202. ASD 2876.
Giebel; Leonhardt Consort. *With* Cantata 203. SAWT 9465.
Telefunken S 9465.
Speiser; Württemberg Chamber Orch; Ewerhart. *With* Cantata 204. †TV 34127S; Turnabout 34127.
211 Schweiget stille, plaudert nicht
Hausmann, Equiluz, Egmond; Vienna Concentus Musicus; Harnoncourt. *With* Cantata 212. *Not part of complete edition.*
SAWT 9515; Telefunken S 9515.
Speiser, Jochims, Ocker; Württemberg Chamber Orch; Ewerhart. *With* Cantata 203. TV 34071S; Turnabout 34071.
212 Mer hahn en neue Oberkeet
Hausmann, Egmond; Vienna Concentus Musicus; Harnoncourt. *With* Cantata 211. *Not part of complete edition.* SAWT 9515; Telefunken S 9515.
Buckel, Ocker; Württemberg Chamber Och; Ewerhart. *With* Cantata 202. † TV 34042S; Turnabout 34042.

ORATORIOS, MASSES, MOTETS, PASSIONS
Christmas oratorio
Treble soloists from Vienna Boys' Choir, Esswood, Equiluz, Nimsgern; Vienna Boys' Choir, Chorus Viennensis; Vienna Concentus Musicus; Harnoncourt. SKH 25 (3 recs); SKH 25T (3 recs).
Ameling, Watts, Pears, Krause; Lübecker Kantorei; Stuttgart Chamber Orch; Münchinger. SET 346-8; London 1386 (3 recs). excerpts 26128.
Ameling, Fassbaender, Laubenthal, Prey; Tölzer Boys' Choir; Bavarian Radio Chorus & Orch; Jochum. 6703037 (3 recs); Phillips 6703037 (3 recs).
Easter Oratorio
Ameling, Watts, Krenn, Krause; Vienna Academy Choir; Stuttgart Chamber Orch; Münchinger. SET 398; London 26100.

Magnificat
   Donath, Bernat-Klein, Finnila, Schreier, McDaniel; South
German Madrigal Choir; German Bach Soloists; Gönnenwein.
Includes Bach's original Christmas interpolations. † BACH
1183.
   Ameling, Bork, Watts, Krenn, Krause; Vienna Academy
Choir; Stuttgart Chamber Orch; Münchinger. *With* Cantata
10. SXL 6400; London 26103.
   Popp, Baker, Tear, Hemsley; New Phil Chorus & Orch;
Barenboim. *With* Bruckner. Te Deum. ASD 2533; Angel S
38815.
Mass in B minor
   Palmer, Watts, Tear, Rippon; Amor Artis Chorale; English
Chamber Orch; Somary. * VSD 71190 (3 recs); Vanguard
71190-2.
   Ameling, Minton, Watts, Krenn, Krause; Vienna Singaka-
demie Chorus; Stuttgart Chamber Orch; Münchinger. SET
477-8; London 1287 (2 recs).
   Hausmann, Liyama, Watts, Equiluz, Egmond; Vienna Boys'
Choir; Vienna Concentus Musicus; Harnoncourt. SKH 20.
(3 recs); SKH 20 (3 recs).
Mass in G minor (235), Mass in G major (236)
   Eathorne, Esswood, Langridge, Roberts; Richard Hickox
Singers & Orch; Hickox. ZRG 829.
Motets—Complete
   Regensburg Choir, Vienna Capella Academica; Hamburg Brass
Ensemble; Schneidt. 2708031 (2 recs); ARC 2708031 (2 recs).
Motets
*225 Singet dem Herrn ein neues Lied; 227 Jesu Meine Freude;
229 Komm, Jesu, komm*
   King's College Choir Cambridge; Willcocks. * HQS 1144.
*226 Der Geist hilft unsrer; 228 Fürchte dich nicht; 230
Lobet den Herrn*
   King's College Choir Cambridge; Willcocks. *With* Cantata
147. * HQS 1254; Angel S 36804.
St John Passion—English versions
   Harper, Hodgson, Pears, Tear, Howell, Shirley-Quirk;

Wandsworth School Boys Choir; English Chamber Orch; Britten.
SET 531-3; London 13104 (3 recs).

Harwood, Watts, Pears, Young, Ward, Alan; King's College
Choir; Philomusica of London; Willcocks. * GOS 628-30.

St John Passion—German versions

Ameling, Hamari, Ellenbeck, Hollweg, Ahrans, Prey; Stuttgart Hymnus Boys' Choir; Stuttgart Chamber Orch; Münchinger.
SET 590-2.

Equiluz, Hoff, Egmond, Villisech, Schneeweis; Vienna Boys'
Choir; Chorus Viennensis; Vienna Concentus Musicus; Gilles-
berger. SKH 19 (3 recs); SKH 19 (3 recs).

St Matthew Passion

Esswood, Sutcliffe, Bowman, Equiluz, Rogers, Ridderbusch,
Egmond, Schopper; Vienna Boys' Choir, Regensburg Cathedral
Boys' Choir; King's College Cambridge Men's Choir; Vienna
Concentus Musicus; Harnoncourt, Willcocks. SAWT 9572-5;
Telefunken S 9572-5.

Ameling, Höffgen, Pears, Wunderlich, Prey, Krause, Blanken-
burg, Messthaler; Stuttgart Hymnus Boys' Choir; Stuttgart
Chamber Orch; Münchinger. SET 288-91, exerpts SXL 6272;
London 1431 (4 recs), exerpts 26008.

Schwarzkopf, Ludwig, Pears, Gedda, Fischer-Dieskau, Berry;
Boys of Hampstead Parish Church Choir; Philharmonia Choir
& Orch; Klemperer. SLS 827 (4 recs); Angel S 3599 (5 recs)
exerpts S 36162.

Janowitz, Ludwig, Schreier, Laubenthal, Fischer-Dieskau,
Berry, Diakov; State & Cathedral Boys' Choirs Berlin; Vienna
Singverein; German Opera Chorus Berlin; Karajan. 2530310-3;
DG 2711012 (4 recs).

ORGAN

Bach wrote a very large number of works for the organ. The
arrangement under this heading is slightly different from usual.
There are two sequences of entries. First comes a sequence arranged alphabetically by artist. Under each artist the recordings
selected are listed in order of the maker's British index number.
For each recording the American index number, when available,

follows the British number, together with a list of works on the recording. The second sequence follows the BWV sequence and under each work lists the recordings selected for that work. Only the British index number is given here.

Individual chorales are not listed, but groups such as the Schübler chorales are. Where a miscellaneous collection of chorales has been recorded they are so indicated. Reference should be made to the *Gramophone classical catalogue* for a listing of individual chorales.

All the recordings listed here, as elsewhere in the discography, can be recommended, but the reader's attention is particularly drawn to two complete sets. The first, by Lionel Rogg on Oryx, is in the cheapest price range. The second, by Michel Chapuis on Telefunken, is expensive but beautifully recorded and includes the scores. Volume 10—Das Orgelbüchlein—has yet to be issued. The playing on both sets is very fine.

ORGAN WORKS LISTED BY ARTIST
Benbow
   * 6599368: Preludes and fugues 542, 548, Toccata 564, Toccata and fugue 565.
Biggs
   MQ 31424; M 31424: Preludes and fugues 542, 544-5, Fantasia 572. Fugue on the Creed from Clavierübung Part III 680, Chorale prelude 753.
Chapuis
   BC 25098-T (2 recs); 25098 (2 recs): Trio sonatas 525-30, Fantasia con imitazione 563, Preludes 568-569, Fantasia 570, Fugues 575, 578, Trio 584.
   BC 25099-T (2 recs); 25099 (2 recs): Schübler chorales 645-650, Christmas chorales 696-701 and other miscellaneous chorales.
   BC 25100-T (2 recs); 25100 (2 recs): Preludes and fugues 534, 536-79, 541-3, 545-6.
   BC 25101-T (2 recs); 25101 (2 recs): Preludes and fugues 531-3, 535, 540, 544, 547-550, Fantasia and Fugue 562.

BC 25102-T (2 recs); 25102 (2 recs): Fantasia 573, Fugue 577, Trio 586, Aria 587, Little harmonic labyrinth 591, Concertos 592-6, Chorales 653b, 656, 741, Trio 1027a.

EK6 35081 (2 recs); 25103 (2 recs): Miscellaneous chorales, Partitas 766-8.

EK6 35082 (2 recs); 25104 (2 recs): Prelude and fugue 551, Toccatas 564, 565, 566, Fantasia 572, Fugues 574, 579, Passacaglia 582, Trio 583, Canzona 588, Allabreve 589, Pastorale 590. .

EK6 35083 (2 recs); 25105 (2 recs): Leipzig Chorales 651-668.

EK6 35084 (2 recs); 25105 (2 recs): Clavierübung Part III.

Chorzempa
6500214; 6500214: Preludes and fugues 532, 543, Toccata 565, Passacaglia 582.

6700059 (2 recs); 6700059 (2 recs): Trio sonatas 525-30.

Downes
† G5GC 14024: Prelude and fugue 540, Fugue à la gigue 577, Chorale partita 768, *With* Widor. Toccata.

TPLS 13001-2: Clavierübung Part III.

Heiller
* HM 35 SD; HM 35: Concertos 592-4, 596.

* VCS 10039-40; C 10039-40: Leipzig Chorales, 651-668.

Hurford
ZRG 776-8; ZRG 776-8: Orgelbüchlein 599-644 (with vocal chorales sung by the Alban Singers).

Kraft
† TV 34084S: Christmas chorales 599-612 and others.

Rogg
† BACH 1002: Fugues 575, 577-9, Canzona 588, Allabreve 589, Pastorale 590.

† BACH 1003: Fantasia and fugue 562, Toccata 566, Fantasia 572, Trio 583, Canonic variations 769.

† BACH 1004: Preludes and fugues 534, 539, Chorale preludes 695, 710, 712, 713, 717, 718, 740.

† BACH 1005: Preludes and fugues 538, 540, Toccata 564.

† BACH 1006: Schübler chorales 645-650, miscellaneous chorales.

† BACH 1007-8: Clavierübung Part III.

† BACH 1009: Trio sonatas 525-8.

† BACH 1010: Trio sonatas 529-530; Chorale variations 653b, 720, 727, 733-4, 736-7.

† BACH 1011: Preludes and fugues 541, 543, 547-8.

† BACH 1012: Preludes and fugues 536, 544-6.

† BACH 1013-4: Orgelbüchlein 599-644.

† BACH 1015: Preludes and fugues 531-3, 535, 549, 550.

† BACH 1016: Partitas 766-8.

† BACH 1017-8: Leipzig Chorales 651-668.

* HQS 1293: Concertos 592-4, 596.

† ORYX 1751: Preludes and fugues 537, 542, Toccata 565, Passacaglia 582.

Richter

138907; 138907: Trio sonata 526, Preludes and fugues 532, 542, Toccata 565.

Sanger

† 2555012: Trio sonata 529, Prelude and fugue 542. *With* Franck. Grande pièce symphonique.

Walcha

* 135046: Trio sonatas 525, 530, Prelude & fugue 547, Toccata 565.

138958: Preludes & fugues 534, 542, 544, 552.

198304: 198304: Preludes & fugues 538, 540, Toccata 564, Toccata 565.

2533126; 2533125: Trio sonatas 526-9.

2533140; 2533140: Trio sonatas 525 & 530, Canzona 588, Allabreve 589, 4 Duets 802-5.

2533160; 2533160: Preludes & fugues 532, 535-6, 550, Fugue 578, Pastorale 590.

† 2565002: Prelude & fugue 535, Toccata 565, Pastorale 590, Chorale preludes 608, 639, 700, 727, 734, 736.

Instrumental music

ORGAN WORKS LISTED UNDER SCHMIEDER'S BWV NUMBERS
525-530 Trio sonatas
 Rogg † BACH 1009-10. Chorzempa 6700059 (2 recs).
Walcha 2533126 & 2533140. Chapuis BC 25098-T (2 recs).
525 E flat major
 Walcha * 135046.
526 C minor
 Richter 138907.
529 C major
 Sanger 2555012.
530 G major
Walcha * 135046.
531-552 Preludes and fugues
531 C major
 Chapuis BC 25101-T (2 recs). Rogg † BACH 1015.
532 D major
 Richter 138907. Chapuis BC 25101-T (2 recs). Rogg
† BACH 1015. Chorzempa 6500214. Walcha 2533160.
533 E minor
 Chapuis BC 25101-T (2 recs). Rogg † BACH 1015.
534 F minor
 Walcha 138958. Rogg † BACH 1004. Chapuis BC 25100-T
(2 recs).
535 G minor
 Chapuis BC 25101-T (2 recs). Rogg † BACH 1015. Walcha
† 2565002. Walcha 2533160.
536 A major
 Rogg † BACH 1012. Chapuis BC 25100-T (2 recs). Walcha
2533160.
537 C minor
 Rogg † ORYX 1751. Chapuis BC 25100-T (2 recs).
538 D minor
 Rogg † BACH 1005. Chapuis BC 25100-T (2 recs). Walcha
198304.
539 D minor
 Rogg † BACH 1004. Chapuis BC 25100-T (2 recs).

540 F major
Chapuis BC 25101-T (2 recs). Downes † GSGC 14024. Walcha 198304. Rogg † BACH 1005.
541 G major
Chapuis BC 25100-T (2 recs). Rogg † BACH 1011.
542 G minor
Richter 138907. Sanger † 255012. Benbow *6599368. Biggs MQ 31424. Rogg † ORYX 1751. Walcha 138958. Chapuis BC 25100-T (2 recs).
543 A minor
Chorzempa 6500214. Rogg † BACH 1011. Chapuis BC 25100-T (2 recs).
544 B minor
Chapuis BC 25101-T (2 recs). Biggs MQ 31424. Rogg † BACH 1012.
545 C major
Biggs MQ 31424. Rogg † BACH 1012. Chapuis BC 25100-T (2 recs).
546 C minor
Chapuis BC 25100-T (2 recs). Rogg † BACH 1012.
547 C major
Walcha * 135046. Chapuis BC 25101-T (2 recs). Rogg † BACH 1011.
548 E minor
Chapuis BC 25101-T (2 recs). Benbow * 6599368. Rogg † BACH 1011.
549 C minor
Chapuis BC 25101-T (2 recs). Rogg † BACH 1015.
550 G major
Walcha 2533160. Chapuis BC 25101-T (2 recs). Rogg † BACH 1015.
551 A minor
Chapuis EK6 35082 (2 recs).
552 E flat major (from Clavierübung III)
Walcha 138958. Downes TPLS 13001-2. Chapuis EK6 35084 (2 recs). Rogg † BACH 1007-8.

Fantasias, Toccatas, Passacaglia etc
562 *Fantasia & fugue C minor*
   Chapuis BC 25101-T (2 recs). Rogg † BACH 1003.
563 *Fantasia con imitazione B minor*
   Chapuis BC 25098 (2 recs).
564 *Toccata C major*
   Chapuis EK6 35082 (2 recs). Benbow *6599368. Rogg
† BACH 1005.
565 *Toccata D minor*
   Richter 138907. Chorzempa 6500214. Chapuis EK6
35082 (2 recs). Benbow *6599368. Rogg † ORYX 1751.
Walcha † 2565002. Walcha * 135046. Walcha 198304.
566 *Toccata E major (C major)*
   Chapuis EK6 35082 (2 recs). Rogg † BACH 1003.
568-9 *Preludes G major & A minor, 570 Fantasia C major*
   Chapuis BC 25098-T (2 recs).
572 *Fantasia G major*
   Chapuis EK6 35082 (2 recs). Biggs MQ 31424. Rogg
† BACH 1003.
573 *Fantasia C major (incomplete)*
   Chapuis BC 25102-T (2 recs).
574 *Fugue C minor*
   Chapuis EK6 35082 (2 recs).
575 *Fugue C minor*
   Chapuis BC 25098-T (2 recs). Rogg † BACH 1002.
577 *Fugue G major*
   Chapuis BC 21502-T (2 recs). Rogg † BACH 1002.
Downes † GSGC 14024.
578 *Fugue G minor*
   Chapuis BC 25098-T (2 recs). Walcha 2533160. Rogg
† BACH 1002.
579 *Fugue B minor on a theme by Corelli*
   Chapuis EK6 35082 (2 recs). Rogg † BACH 1002.
582 *Passacaglia C minor*
   Chorzempa 6500214. Chapuis EK6 35082 (2 recs). Rogg
† ORYX 1751.

583 Trio D minor
  Chapuis EK6 35082 (2 recs). Rogg † BACH 1003.
584 Trio G minor
  Chapuis BC 25098-T (2 recs).
586 Trio G major after Telemann, 587 Air F major after Couperin
  Chapuis BC 25102-T (2 recs).
588 Canzona D minor
  Chapuis EK6 35082 (2 recs). Rogg † BACH 1002.
589 Allabreve D major
  Chapuis EK6 35082 (2 recs). Rogg † BACH 1002.
590 Pastorale F major
  Walcha † 2565002. Walcha 2533160. Chapuis EK6
35082 (2 recs). Rogg † BACH 1002.
591 Little harmonic labyrinth
  Chapuis BC 25102-T (2 recs).
592-7 Concertos
  Chapuis BC 25102-T (2 recs).
592-4, 596 Concertos
  Heiller * HM 35 SD. Rogg * HQS 1293.
599-644 Orgelbüchlein
  Hurford ZRG 766-8 (with original vocal chorales sung by
the Alban Singers). Rogg † BACH 1013-4.
599-612, 614, 659, 696-700, 703-4, 710, 722-4, 738 Christmas chorales
  Kraft † TV 34084S.
645-50 Chorales (Schübler)
  Rogg † BACH 1006. Chapuis BC 25099-T (2 recs).
651-668 Leipzig chorales
  Chapuis EK6 35083 (2 recs). Rogg † BACH 1017-8. Heiller
*VCS 10039-40.
669-689 Clavierübung Part III
  Downes TPLS 13001-2. Rogg † BACH 1007-8. Chapuis
EK6 35084 (2 recs).
*696-701, 703-4, 710, 713, 722, 722a, 724, 729, 729a, 732,
732a, 738, 738a Christmas chorales*
  Chapuis BC 25099-T (2 recs).

766-8 Partitas
  Chapuis EK6 35081 (2 recs). Rogg † BACH 1016.
768 Partita G minor
  Downes † GSGC 14024.
769 Canonic variations
  Chapuis BC 25099-T (2 recs). Rogg † BACH 1003.

CLAVIER
French suite 5 G major 816, Chromatic fantasia and fugue D
minor 903, Toccata D major 912, Italian concerto F major
971
  Malcolm (harpsichord) * SDD 272; London 6197.
Two part inventions 772-85, Partita 2 C minor 826, Das wohl-
temperierte Klavier: Prelude C major 846, Chromatic fantasia
and fugue D minor 903, Fantasia C minor 906, Italian concerto
F major 971, Capriccio B flat major 992
  Kirkpatrick (harpsichord) * 2726016 (2 recs).
English suite 2 A minor 807, French suite 6 E major 817, Fan-
tasia C minor 906, Italian concerto F major 971
  Larocha (piano) SXL 6545.
French suite 6 E major 817, Chromatic fantasia and fugue D
minor 903, Fantasia C minor 906, Italian concerto F major 971
  Pearson (harpsichord) † CFP 40049.
Chromatic fantasia and fugue D minor 903, Fantasia and fugue
A minor 904, Capriccio B flat major 992, Suite for lute E minor
996
  Leonhardt SAWT 9571; Telefunken S 9571.
Capriccio B flat 992
  Dreyfus (harpsichord). With French suite nos 5 and 6,
816-7. 2533139; 2533139.
Concertos 972-987
Concertos after Vivaldi 972, 973, 975, 976, 978, 980
  Sartori (harpsichord) * 6580017.
  Sebastyen (harpsichord) † TV 34287 S.
French suites see Suites p126.
Goldberg variations 988
  Malcolm (harpsichord) Includes repeats * SOL 261-2;
Oiseau Lyre S 261-2.

Galling (harpsichord) † TV 34015S; 34015.

Kempff (piano) 139455; 139455.

Richter (harpsichord) *With repeats* 2707057 (2 recs).

Leonhardt (harpsichord) SAWT 9474; Telefunken S 9474.

Inventions, Two and three part 772-801

Ruzickova (harpsichord) Erato ERA 9038.

Partitas 825-30

Richter (harpsichord) KT 11012 (2 recs); Telefunken S 9913-4.

Adlam (harpsichord) † BACH 1200-1.

Suites 806-817

French suites 812-817

Gilbert (harpsichord) HMU 438 (2 recs).

Dreyfus (harpsichord) *With* Capriccio 992. 2533138-9; 2533138-9.

Dart (clavichord) * SOL 60039; 60039.

Well-tempered clavier 846-893

Cole (piano) † SAGA 5151-6.

LUTE

Suite E minor 996: Allemande, bourrée, Prelude C minor 999, Fugue G minor 1000, Suite E major 1006: loure, gavotte, minuets 1 and 2, gigue, Suite A major 1007 (complete)

Gerwig (lute) † BACH 1202.

CHAMBER MUSIC

Flute sonata A minor 1013, 6 sonatas for flute & clavier 1030-1035

Preston (flute), Pinnock (harpsichord), Savall (viola da gamba) CRD 1014-5.

Solo violin sonatas and partitas 1001-1006

Grumiaux SAL 3472-4; 835198-200.

Szeryng 2709028 (3 recs); 2709028 (3 recs).

Suk SLS 818 (3 recs).

Violin & clavier sonatas 1014-9

David Oistrakh (violin), Pischner (harpsichord) *2726002.

Instrumental music

Cello suites 1007-12
   Tortelier * SL3 798 (3 recs).
   Fournier SAPM 198186-8; 198186-8.
   Casals RLS 712 (3 recs).
   Clément † OLS 133-4; Oiseau Lyre S 133-4.
3 Viola da gamba & clavier sonatas 1027-9
   Dupré (gamba), Dart (harpsichord) † OLS 157.

CONCERTOS
Clavier
1-7 (1052-9)
   Kipnis (harpsichord); London Strings; Marriner. * 77335
(4 recs); M4-30540 (4 recs).
1 D minor 1052
   Ashkenazy (piano); London Sym; Zinman. *With* Chopin.
Piano Concerto no 2. SXL 6174; London 6440.
1 D minor 1052, 2 E major 1053
   Malcolm (harpsichord); Menuhin Festival Orch; Menuhin.
ASD 3007; Angel S 37010.
3 D major 1054, 4 A major 1055, 6 F major 1057
   Malcolm (harpsichord): Menuhin Festival orch; Menuhin.
ASD 2713. Angel S 36790.
5 F major 1056, 7 G minor 1058
   Malcolm (harpsichord); Menuhin Festival Orch; Menuhin.
With concertos for two claviers. 1060-1. ASD 2647;
Angel S-36762.
2 claviers, 1 C minor 1060, 2 C major 1061
   Malcolm, Preston (harpsichord); Menuhin Festival Orch;
Menuhin. *With* Clavier concertos 5 and 7. ASD 2647; Angel
S 36762.
2 claviers, 2 C major 1061
   Haskil, Anda (pianos); Philharmonia Orch; Galliena. *With*
Mozart. Concerto for two pianos. * SXLP 30175.
*3 claviers, 1 D minor (1063), 2 C major (1064), 4 claviers A
minor (1065)*
   Galling, Bilgram, Lehrndorfer, Stolze (harpsichords); Mainz

Chamber Orch; Kehr. † TV 34106S; 34290-4 (*With* other Bach concertos).

VIOLIN

1 A minor 1041, 2 E major 1042, 2 violins D minor 1043
Menuhin, Ferras; Bath Festival Chamber Orch; Menuhin. ASD 346.

Melkus, Rantos; Vienna Capella Academica. 2533075; 2533075.

D Oistrakh, I Oistrakh; Vienna Sym Orch; Royal Phil Orch; Goossens. 138820; 138820.

Michelucci, Ayo; I Musici. 658021.

Flute, violin & clavier A minor 1044, 3 violins (arr from 3 clavier concerto) D major
Hörtzsch (flute), Bosse (violin), Kästner (harpsichord); Gläss, Nietner (violins); Leipzig Gewandhaus Orch; Bosse. * 6580058.

Brandenburg Concertos 1-6 (1046-51)
Württemberg Chamber Orch; Faerber. † TV 34044-5; 34044-5.

Collegium Aureum. *Using original instruments.* BAC 3007-8; VICS 6023 (2 recs).

Bath Festival Chamber Orch; Menuhin. ASD 3278; Angel S 3787

English Chamber Orch; Britten. SET 410-1; London 2225 (2 recs).

Overtures (Suites) 1-4 (1066-1069)
Academy of St Martin in the Fields; Marriner ZRG 687-8 ZRG 687-8.

Collegium Aureum. *Using original instruments.* BAC 3009-10; BASF 20332 (2 recs).

English Chamber Orch; Leppard. 6500067-8; 639792 (2 recs).

Vienna Concentus Musicus; Harnoncourt. SAWT 9509-10; Telefunken S 9509-10.

MUSICAL OFFERING, THE ART OF FUGUE
The Musical Offering 1079
 Stuttgart Chamber Orch; Münchinger. * SDD 310; STS
15063.
 Vienna Concentus Musicus; Harnoncourt. SAWT 9565;
Telefunken S 9565.
 Büchner, Gunter (violins), Meinecke (viola), Kiskait (cello),
Nicolet (flute), Bilgram, Richter (harpsichord). 198320;
198320.
 Munich Instrumental Ensemble. † TV 34451S; 34451.
The Art of fugue
 Rogg (organ). SLS 782 (2 recs); Angel S 3766 (2 recs).
 Stuttgart Chamber Orch; Münchinger. SET 303-4; 2215.
(2 recs).
 Walcha (organ). 2708002; 2708002.
The Art of Fugue (arr Isaacs)
 Philomusica of London; Malcolm. * SDD 356-7; London
5421-2.

Index

No entries are included for the selected recordings of Bach's music

Abraham, G 62

Agricola, J F 50, 54

Ahle, J G 17

Alain, O 106

d'Albert, E 96, 97, 101

Albert, M 91

Aldrich, P *Ornamentation in J S Bach's organ works* 69

Alexander, A 100

Allen, Sir H 88

Altmann, W 105

Altnickol, J C 50

Alwyn, W 88, 97

Amalia, Princess, of Sachsen-Poland 43, 44

Ameln, K 76, 93, 94

Andrews, H K 97

Arnstadt, 'New Church' of St Boniface 14, 15

Art of Fugue 50

Art of Fugue. A guide to the new concert version by W Goehr and M Seiber (Seiber) 71

Art of J S Bach (Dickinson) 62

Atkins, E 92

Atkins, Sir I 84-86, 92, 95

Auer, L 102

Augustus I, Elector of Saxony and King of Poland 37

Aveling, C 84-86

Babin, V 95

Bach, Anna Magdalena 30, 45-47, 51

Bach, Carl Philipp Emanuel 7-11, 21, 24, 25, 36, 40, 46, 47, 50, 51, 54, 59

Bach, Catharina Dorothea 21, 25

Bach, Georg Christoph 9

Bach, Gottlieb Friedrich 8

Bach, Johann Ambrosius 10

Bach, Johann August 40

Bach, Johann Bernhard 14

Bach, Johann Christian 40, 51, 52

Bach, Johann Christoph 9-12, 14, 18, 25

Bach, Johann Elias 45, 46, 49

Bach, Johann Ernst 16

Bach, Johann Gottfried Bernhard 40, 41

Bach, Johann Jacob 11, 12

Bach, Johann Ludwig 8

Bach, Johann Michael 18

Bach, J S *Elementary instruction in figured bass* 55

Bach, Johann Sebastian *Origin of the Bach family of musicians* 7-9, 11

Bach, Johann Sebastian (the younger) 50

Bach, Liessgen 50

Bach, Maria Barbara 15, 17, 18, 21, 25, 47

Bach, Regine Susanna 52

Bach, Vitus 8

Bach, Wilhelm Friedmann 8, 23, 24, 38, 45, 48, 54, 55

Bach (Boughton) 58

Bach (Holst) 61

Bach (Meynell) 59, 60

Bach. A biography (Terry) 59

Bach. A pictorial biography (Neumann) 60

Bach. The cantatas and oratorios (Terry) 64

Bach. The historical approach (Terry) 59

Bach. The Magnificat, Lutheran Masses and Motets (Terry) 64

Bach. The Mass in B minor (Terry) 64

Bach. The Passions (Terry) 64

Bach and Handel. The consumation of the baroque in music (Davison) 61, 62

Bach Archiv, Leipzig 74

Bach aria index (Whaples) 66

130

Bach book for Harriet Cohen 79
Bach cantatas (Westrup) 64
Bach chorale texts in English translation, etc (Drinker) 63
Bach family. Seven generations of creative genius (Geiringer) 60
Bach Gesellschaft 73
Bach-Jahrbuch 53, 74
Bach organ music (Williams) 68
Bach reader. A life of J S Bach in letters and documents (David & Mendel) 53, 54
Bach the borrower (Carrell) 63
Bach's Brandenburg concertos (Carrell) 67
Bach's Brandenburg concertos (Fuller-Maitland) 67
Bach's fugal works (Dickinson) 62
Bach's Mass in B minor (Terry) 64
Bach's orchestra (Terry) 66
Bach's organ works (Hull) 67
Bach's organ works (Keller) 67
Bach's ornaments (Emery) 69, 70
Bach's world (Chiapusso) 60
The Bachs, 1500-1850 (Young) 60
Background of passion music. J S Bach and his predecessors (Smallman) 63
Baker, H E 91, 92
Baldwin Wallace College 54
Bantock, Sir G 96
Barge, W 102
Bargiel, W 94
Bartholomew, W 93, 94
Bartok, B 100, 101
Bauer, H 99, 105
Baumgartner, R 105
Bax, Sir A 79
Beckett, J 97
Bell, C 55
Bellstedt, J 17
Bergmann, W 90, 91
Besseler, H 77
Best, W T 95
Bibliographical Services Division of the British Library 78
Biggs, E P 80, 106

Birnbaum, J A 44
Bischoff, H 98, 100, 101
Bizony, C The family of Bach 60
Blankenburg, W 76, 93
Bliss, Sir A 79
Blume, F 103
Blume, F Two centuries of Bach. An account of changing tastes 61
Bodky, E The interpretation of Bach's keyboard works 70
Böhm, G 12, 14, 16
Born, J 51
Boughton, R Bach 58
John Sebastian Bach 58
Boult, Sir A and Emery, W The St Matthew Passion. Its preparation and performance 63
Borwick, L 96-98
Bowen, Y 96
Bragiotti, M 96
Brandenburg concertos 25
Bream, J 101
Breikoff, W 100
Bridge, Sir J F 95
British catalogue of music 78
Brooke, H 101
Bruger, H D 101
Brühl, Count H von 50, 51
Bulman, B E 89, 94
Bülow, H von 99
Buffardin, P 11, 12
Bunk, G 106
Burney, C 37, 54, 61
Busch, A 103
Busoni, F 95, 96, 98-102, 104
Buszin, W 93, 94
Butler, M E 85
Buxtehude, D 12, 15, 16, 56

Cailliet, L 97, 98
Cantatas of Johann Sebastian Bach, sacred and secular (Whittaker) 64
Capriccio on the departure of his beloved brother 11
Carl Friedrich, Prince, of Anhalt-Bernburg 27

Carrell, N *Bach the borrower* 63
  Bach's Brandenburg concertos 67
Carse, A 105
Casella, A 101, 102
*Catalog of the Emilie and Karl
  Riemenschneider Bach
  Library* (Kenney) 54
Chambers, H A 91
Champeil, J 102
Charles III, King of the two
  Sicilies 43
Charlotte Friederich, Princess,
  of Nassau-Siegen 28
Chasins, A 97
Chiapusso, J *Bach's world* 60
Chorale preludes of J S Bach
  (Taylor) 68
Christian, Duke, of Sachsen-
  Weissenfels 22
Christian Ludwig, Margrave of
  Brandenburg 25
Christmas oratorio 38, 39
Chronicle of Leipzig 51
'Chronology of the vocal works
  of J S Bach' (Dürr) 53
Church cantatas of J S Bach
  (Robertson) 65
*Clavierbüchlein vor Anna
  Magdalena Bach* 26
*Clavierbüchlein vor Wilhelm
  Friedemann Bach* 24
Cohen, H 81, 89, 97
Coleman, H 96
Collegium musicum 32, 39, 44
Colles, H C 87
*Commentary on Book 1 (Book 2)
  of the forty-eight preludes
  and fugues of Johann Sebastian
  Bach* (Macpherson) 70
*Companion to Bach's Orgel-
  büchlein* (Hunt) 69
Companion to the Art of fugue
  (Tovey) 71
*Compositional process of
  J S Bach* (Marshall) 63
Connor, Sister M J B *Gregorian
  chant and mediaeval hymn
  tunes in the works of
  J S Bach* 66

Copeland, F P 89
Corelli, A 15
Craster, R M 84
Craxton, H 105
Der Critische Musicus 43
Crussard, C 103
Czerny, C 99, 100, 106

Dadelsen, G von 76, 100
Dart, T 66
David, F 100, 103, 104
David, H 99
David, H T 106
  *J S Bach's musical offering.
  History, interpretation and
  analysis* 71
David, H T & Mendel, A *The
  Bach reader* 53, 54
David, J N 105
Davison, A T *Bach and Handel.
  The consummation of the
  baroque in music* 61, 62
Davisson, W 99, 102-4
Day, J *The literary background
  to Bach's cantatas* 65
Debussy, C A 103
Dehn, S W 104, 105
Délacluse, U 103
Dendorf, C 36
Deutsch, O E 96
Devrient, E 54
Deyling, S 42
Diack, J M 91
Dickinson, A E F *The art of
  J S Bach* 62
  Bach's fugal works 62
Diener, H 106
Dieupart, C 13
Döbereiner, C 103
Dolmetsch, A 70
Donington, R *Tempo and
  rhythm in Bach's organ
  music* 69
Dörffel, A *Thematisches Verzeich-
  nis der Instrumentalwerke von
  Joh Seb Bach* 73
Dounis, D C 102
Dresden, Church of our Lady 47
  Church of St Sophia 37

132

Drese, J S 22
Drinker, H S 82, 84, 89, 90
  *The Bach chorale texts in English
    translation, etc* 63
Duncan, C H S 96, 97
Dürr, A 34, 64, 74-7, 86-93
  'Chronology of the vocal works
    of J S Bach' 53
  'New light on Bach' 79
Dupré, M 95
Dykes-Bower, Sir J 95
Dymond, E 59

Editions:
  Art of fugue 106
  Cantatas 79-92
  Chamber music 102, 103
  Chorales 94
  Clavier works 98-101
  Hymns 94
  Lute works 101, 102
  Masses, passions, oratorios 92,
    93
  Motets 93, 94
  Musical offering 105-106
  Orchestral works 104, 105
  Organ works 94-98
  Psalm 94
  Songs and arias 94
Edler, R 77
Ehret, W 88, 93
*Eight short preludes and
  fugues* (Emery) 68
Eilmar, G C 19
Eisenach, St George's Church 10
Eitelwein, J F 39
*Elementary instruction in
  figured bass* (J S Bach) 55
Eleonore Wilhelmine, Duchess,
  of Sachsen-Merseburg 22
Elgar, Sir E 96
Emery, W 71, 82, 85, 95, 96
  Bach's ornaments 69, 70
  Eight short preludes and fugues
    ('Notes on Bach's organ
    works') 68
  *Six sonatas for two manuals
    and pedal* ('Notes on Bach's
    organ works') 68

Emery, W (cont'd)
  see also Boult, Sir A
England, P 80, 81, 83, 86, 88
Eppstein, H 103
Erdmann, G 12, 13, 35
Erk, L 94
Ernesti, J A 40, 42
Ernesti, J H 29, 34
Ernst August, Duke, of Sachsen-
  Weimar, 20, 22

Family of Bach (Bizony) 60
Fauré, G 101
Faustina (Bordoni) 37
Feldhaus, M 15
Ferguson, H 102, 103
Fischer, E 99-101
Fischer, W 77
Flesch, C 102, 104
Fleury, L 102
Forbes, W 88, 103, 104
Forkel, J N 11, 12, 23, 36, 47-
  49, 51, 54
  *Johann Sebastian Bach. His life,
    art and times* 54
*The '48'. Bach's Wohl-temperiertes
  Clavier* (Fuller-Maitland) 70
*Forty-eight preludes and fugues
  of J S Bach* (Gray) 70
Foster, A 98, 99
Fournier, P 103
Fox-Strangways, A H 90
Franck, S 20-23
Franz, R 83
Frederick, the Great, King in
  Prussia 42, 47-49
Frederick Augustus II, Elector of
  Saxony and King of Poland
  37-39, 43
Freeman, R 90
Frescobaldi, G 23
Friederica Henrietta, Princess,
  of Anhalt-Bernburg 27
Friskin, J 86, 98, 100
Froberger, J J 12
Frohne, J A 19
Frotscher, G 95, 105
*Fugitive notes on certain cantatas and
  motets of J S Bach* (Whittaker) 64

Fuller-Maitland, J A 55
Bach's Brandenburg concertos 67
The '48'. Bach's Wohltemperier-
tes Clavier 70
The keyboard suites of J S Bach
71

Gaillard, F 103
Gál, H 104, 106
Geehl, H 102
Geiringer, I 60
Geiringer, K 10, 104
The Bach family. Seven
generations of creative genius
60
Johann Sebastian Bach. The
culmination of a great era 60
Symbolism in the music of Bach
60
Gerber, H N 24
Gerber, R 76, 102
Gesner, J M 34-36, 39, 40
Geyersbach, J H 15
Godman, S 61
Godowsky, L 103
Goehr, W 79
Goldberg variations 46
Goldsworthy, W 88
Goodrich, W 67
Gott ist mein König 18
Gottes Zeit ist die allerbeste
Zeit 18
Gould, G 101
Grace, H *The listener's guide*
to the organ music of Bach 67
The organ works of Bach 67
Grainger, P 91, 96
Gräser, W 105
Graupner, C 27, 28
Gray, C *The forty-eight*
preludes and fugues of
J S Bach 70
Gregorian chant and mediaeval
hymn tunes in the works of
J S Bach (Connor) 66
Greitz, W 105
Grey, C 93
Griepenkerl, F C 94, 99

Grigny, N de 13
Grischkat, H 81, 82, 84, 86-9, 92
Grümmer, P 99, 103
Gui, V 89, 90, 97

Haan, S de 61
Halle, Bach's visit to 21
Hambourg, J 102
Hamburg, St James's Church 25
Handbook to the performance of
the 48 preludes and fugues of
J S Bach, etc (Rothschild) 71
Handel, G F 23, 37
Hannam, W *Notes on the church*
cantatas of John Sebastian
Bach 64
Harrassowitz 93
Harrer, G 51
Harris, J 96
Harris, R 96, 106
Harris, Sir W H 96
Hasse, J A 37
Haussmann, E G 8
Hausswald, G 76, 102
Hawkins, Sir J 54
Haywood, E 96
Heaps, P 96
Heitmann, J J 25
Hercules auf dem Scheidewege 38
Hewitt, H 68
Heller, K 77
Hellmann, D 89, 90, 92-4
Hellmesberger, J 102
Helms, M 74, 75
Henrici, C F *see* Picander
Herda, E 12
Hermann, E 104
Hess, Dame M 88, 97
Higgs, J 95
Hiller, Cantor 45
Hindemith, P *Johann Sebastian*
Bach: heritage and obligation
63
Hinrichsen's eighth music book 69
Hoffmann, A 99
Hoffmann-Erbrecht, L 92
Holst, I *Bach* 61
Honegger, A 101

Horn, P 80, 81, 83, 85, 86, 88-90
Horrocks, H 97
Howe, M 88, 91
Hudson, F 75
Hughes, E 96, 101, 103, 104
Hull, A E 95
  Bach's organ works 67
Hunt, E H 89, 91, 93
Hunt, J E A companion to Bach's Orgelbüchlein 69

Ich hatte viel Bekümmernis 21
Interpretation of Bach's keyboard works (Bodky) 70
Introduction to the music of Johann Sebastian Bach (Mann) 62
Inventions 24
Irmer, O von 101
Italian concerto 44

J S Bach (Pirro) 56
J S Bach as a biblical interpreter (Scheide) 66
J S Bach's musical offering. History, interpretation and analysis (David) 71
Jackson, J B 105
Jacob, B 61
Jacob, G 104
Jacobsen, M 102, 103
Jacobson, M 91
Jacques, R 81, 88
  'Jesu joy of man's desiring' 88
Jesus nahm zu sich die Zwölfe 28
Job, Syndicus 33
Joh Seb Bach's cantata texts, sacred and secular (Terry) 65
Johann Ernst, Duke, of Sachsen-Weimar 15, 19, 20, 97
Johan Georg, Duke, of Sachsen-Weissenfels 14
Johann Sebastian Bach (Poole) 56
Johann Sebastian Bach: heritage and obligation (Hindemith) 63
Johann Sebastian Bach Institute, Göttingen 74

Johann Sebastian Bach. His life, art and times (Forkel) 54
Johann Sebastian Bach. His work and influence on the music of Germany (Spitta) 55
Johann Sebastian Bach. The culmination of a great era (Geiringer) 60
Johann Sebastian Bach. The organist and his works for organ (Hull) 67
Johann Sebastian Bach. The story of the development of a great personality (Parry) 58, 59
John Sebastian Bach (Boughton) 58
Jonas, O 98
Jones, I 81, 87

Kahn, E 87
Karg-Elert, S 99
Kayserling, Baron C von 46-48
Keller, H 94, 95, 98, 99, 101
  Bach's organ works 67, 68
Kenney, S W Catalog of the Emilie and Karl Riemenschneider Bach Library 54
Keyboard suites of J S Bach (Fuller-Maitland) 71
Kilian, D 75, 76, 90
Kinsky, G 96
Kirkpatrick, R 99, 100
Klemm, J 41
Klengel, J 103
Klotz, H 76
Koch, C 96
Koch, J W 45
Kodály, Z 99, 102
Kollmann, A F C 37
Kortschak, H 103
Kramer, C 97
Krause, G T 41
Krause, J G 41
Krebs, J T 33
Kreisler, F 103
Kretschmer, E 92
Kreutz, A 101
Kroll, F 101

Kuhnau, J 27, 36
Kulka, E 87

Lämmerhirt, A C 26
Lämmerhirt, E 10
Lämmerhirt, T 26
Landshoff, L 91, 100, 103, 105
Langrish, V 96
Lanon 92, 93
Leipzig, Church of St Nicholas
   30, 32, 42
  Church of St Peter 30
  New Church 30
  St Thomas's Church 7
  Thomas School 27-31
Leipzig song book 32
Leopold, Prince, of Anhalt-
   Cöthen 22, 25, 27, 28, 32
Le Roy, R 102
Letters of Samuel Wesley . . .
   relating to the introduction
   into this country of the works
   of J S Bach 61
Lewis, Sir A 106
Ley, H G 97
Leyden, R von 103
Libera, S della 97
Lipatti, D 91, 97
Listener's guide to the organ
   music of Bach (Grace) 67
Liszt, F 96, 99
Literary background to Bach's
   cantatas (Day) 65
Lohmann, H 94, 106
Longo, A 101
Lost tradition in music
   (Rothschild) 71
Lübeck, Bach's visit to 15, 16
Lubrich, F 94
Ludewig, B D 33
Luedke, H 95
Lully, J B 13
Lüneburg, Bach's visit to 12, 13
  St John's Church 14
  St Michael's Church 12
Lunn, J 93
Lunow, A 106
Luther, M 31

Macpherson, S *A commentary on*
   Book 1 (Book 2) of the forty-
   eight preludes and fugues of
   Johann Sebastian Bach 70
Mahler, G 105
Mainardi, E 103
Mandyczewski, E 104
Mann, W *Introduction to the music*
   of Johann Sebastian Bach 62
Marcello, A 99
Maria-Josepha, Queen-Electress,
   of Sachsen-Poland 38
Markevich, I 107
Marshall, R L *The compositional*
   process of J S Bach 63
Martin, F 94
Mason, W 100
Mass in B minor 37, 38, 46
Mayer, von 45
Melodic index to the works of
   Johann Sebastian Bach (Payne) 73
Mendel, A 75, 90, 92
   see David, H T & Mendel
Mendelssohn, F 7, 54, 79, 102
Menke, W *History of the trumpet*
   of Bach and Handel 62
Meynell, Lady E *Bach* 59, 60
Middelschulte, W 99
Miller, R 96, 97
Millman, W H 83
Mizler, L C 44, 50
Morgan, O 101
Mouquet, J 102
Moyse, L 102
Mugellini, B 98, 99, 101
Mühlhausen, Church of St Balise
   17, 18
  St Mary's Church 40
Music of Bach (Terry) 62
Der musikalische Patriot 25
Müller, G 104
Müller von Asow, E H 103
Murrill, H 85
Musical offering 49
Musical times 79

Naumann, E 94
Neue Bach Ausgabe 74-77

Neue Bach Gesellschaft 73, 74
Neue Zeitschrift für Musik 7
Neumann, W 74, 75, 77, 87, 91,
    93, 94, 103
Bach. A pictorial biography 61
'New light on Bach' (Dürr) 79
Newman, E 57
Nicholson, R 100
Nies-Berger, E 95
Norton, M D H 106
*Notes on the church cantatas of
    John Sebastian Bach* (Hannam)
    64

Ochs, S 86
Odom, J 96
Oistrakh, D 104
Orel, A 104
'Organ of Bach' (Sumner) 69
Organ works of Bach (Grace) 67
*Origin of the Bach family of
    musicians* (J S Bach) 7, 8, 9
Ormandy, E 88
*Ornamentation in J S Bach's
    organ works* (Aldrich) 69
Oubradous, F 105

Pachelbel, J 11, 12
Parry, Sir C H H *Johann
    Sebastian Bach. The story of
    the development of a great
    personality* 58, 59
Partitas 36
Payne, M de F *Melodic index to
    the works of Johann Sebastian
    Bach* 73
Petri, E 91, 98, 99, 101, 102
Petzold, C F 34
Picander (pseudonym of
    C F Henrici) 32
Pierne, G 96
Pillney, K H 106
Pinkman, D 93
Pirro, A *J S Bach* 56
    *Johann Sebastian Bach. The
    organist and his works for
    organ* 67
Plater, D 96

Plath, W 76
Pointer, J 82-84, 86, 88
Poole, R L *Johann Sebastian Bach*
    56
Potsdam, Bach's visit to 47-49
Praetorius, M 13
*Preise dein Glücke, gesegnetes
    Sachsen* 39
Prelude for beginners 24
Prostakoff, V 96
Prout, E 88

Quantz, J J 37
Quintilian 36

Rachmaninov, S 102
Radeke, W 92, 105
Rambach, J A 16
Ramin, G 97
Raphael, G 89, 93
Ratcliffe, D 81
Reeves, B 100
Reger, M 86, 96, 97, 99, 100, 102,
    104, 105
Reinecke, C 98-100
Reinken, J A 14, 16
Resphigi, O 96, 97
Reutsch, J E 8
Rheinberger, J 99
Riemenschneider, A *Some aspects
    of the use of flutes in the sacred
    choral and vocal works of
    Johann Sebastian Bach* 66
Robb, S 91
Robertson, A *The church cantatas
    of J S Bach* 65
Roitsch, F 94, 98, 99, 104
Röntgen, J 96
Roper, E S 87
Rosanoff, M R & L 103
Rösler, F 85, 92, 93
Rösler, G 81
Roth, H 92, 98
Rothsay, W G 81
Rothschild, F *A handbook to the
    performance of the 48 preludes
    and fugues of J S Bach, etc* 71
    The lost tradition in music 71

137

Rowley, A 96
Ruthardt, A 101, 104

Saar, L V 99
Sachs, H 26
St John passion 28
St Matthew passion 29, 52,
    54, 79
St Matthew passion. Its prepara-
    tion and performance (Boult
    & Emery) 63
Samaroff, O 97
Sangerhausen, Church of
    St James 14
Sauer, E von 96, 99, 100
Savill, M 56
'Schafe könner sicher weiden' 91
Scheiber, J A 43, 44, 61
Scheide, W H J S Bach as a
    biblical interpreter 66
Schenker, H 98
Schering, A 80-92, 99, 100,
    104, 105
Schleicht, spielende Welle 39
Schmid-Linder, A 100, 102
Schmieder, W Thematisch-
    systematisches Verzeichnis
    der musikalischen Werke von
    Johann Sebastian Bach 72, 73
Schmitz, H-P 76, 102
Schneider, M 92, 105
Schoenberg, A 96, 97
Schreck, G 102
Schreiber, F C 96
Schubart, J M 23
Schuberth 82
Schübler, J G 47, 49
Schulze, H-J 77, 98
Schumann, G 92
Schumann, R A 102
Schwedler, M 102
Schweitzer, A 95
    J S Bach 57, 58
Scott, C 100
Scott, C K 89
Seiber, M 105
    The art of fugue. A guide to the
    new concert version by
    W Goehr and M Seiber 71

Seidlhofer, B G 106
Seiffert, M 94, 106
Selle, T de la 13
'Sheep may safely graze' 79, 91
Silbermann, G 47, 48
Siloti, A 98, 104
Six sonatas for two manuals and
    pedal (Emery) 68
Smallman, B The background of
    passion music. J S Bach and
    his predecessors 63
Smend, F 75, 92-4, 98
Society of Musical Sciences 8, 44
Soldan, K 99, 102, 104
Some aspects of the use of flutes
    in the sacred choral and vocal
    works of Johann Sebastian
    Bach (Riemenschneider) 66
Spenersche Zeitung 48, 51
Spiro 102
Spitta, P 79
    Johann Sebastian Bach. His work
    and influence on the music of
    Germany 55, 56
Stainer, C 102
Stanford, Sir C 92
Stauber, J L 18
Steger, A 33
Steglich, R 99, 101
Stein, F 94
Stein, J M 87
Steinberg, M 102
Steinitz, P 81, 93
Stephenson, Mr 54
Sterndale-Bennett, Sir W 92
Stieglitz, C L 51
Stokowski, L 91
Straube, K 92, 94, 96
Stravinsky, I 98
Streatfeild, R A Modern music and
    musicians 61
Der Streit zwischen Phoebus und
    Pan 44
Strub, M 104
Style of John Sebastian Bach's
    chorale preludes (Taylor) 68
Sumner, W L 'The organ of
    Bach' 109
Svečenski, L 103

138

Symbolism in the music of Bach (Geiringer) 60
Szigeti, J 104, 105

Tamme, C *Thematisches Verzeichnis der Vocalwerke von Joh Seb Bach* 73
Tausig, C 96
Taylor, J 51
Taylor, S de B 98
Chorale preludes of J S Bach 68
Teichmüller, K 104
Telemann, G P 27, 32, 99
Tempo and rhythm in Bach's organ music (Donington) 69
Terry, C S 54, 58, 74, 81-84, 86-88, 91, 92, 94
Bach. A biography 59
Bach. The cantatas and oratorios 64
Bach. The historical approach 59
Bach. The magnificat, Lutheran masses and motets 64
Bach. The mass in B minor 64
Bach. The passions 64
Joh Seb Bach's cantata texts sacred and secular 65
Bach's mass in B minor 64
Bach's orchestra 66
The music of Bach 62
Tertis, L 102, 104
Tessmer, M 76
Thematisch-systematisches Verzeichnis der musikalischen Werke von Johann Sebastian Bach (Schmieder) 72, 73
Thematisches Verzeichnis der Instrumentalwerke von Joh Seb Bach (Dörffel) 73
Thematisches Verzeichnis der Vocalwerke von Joh Seb Bach (Tamme) 73
Thorne, E H 85
Tippett, Sir M 90, 91
Todt, J A W 102
Tönet ihr Pauken 38
Tortelier, P 103
Töttcher, H 104

Tovey, Sir D F 101, 106
Companion to the art of fugue 71
Towsey, V 96
Trede, H 99
Treitler, L 75
Troutbeck, J 80-83, 85, 86, 88, 92
Tureck, R 98
Tusler, R L *The style of John Sebastian Bach's chorale preludes* 68
Two centuries of Bach (Blume) 61

Vaughan Williams, R 79 98
Vivaldi, A 23, 99
Vogrich, M 98
Vollbach, F 92
Vuataz, R 98, 106

Wackernagel, P 97, 104
Walcha, H 106
Wall, H 99
Walters, 93, 94
Walton, Sir W 79
Was mir behagt 22
Webster, J 75, 90
Weinen, Klagen 23
Wenn wir in hochsten Nöten sein 51
Wanzinger, A 103, 104
Wesley, E 61
Wesley, S 62 *Letter of Samuel Wesley to Mr Jacob relating to the introduction into this country of the works of J S Bach* 61
West, J E 80-83, 87, 93-95
Westrup, Sir J A *Bach cantatas* 65
Whaples, M K *Bach aria index* 66
Whittaker, W G 65, 81, 82, 84-88, 90-93, 97, 105
The cantatas of Johann Sebastian Bach, sacred and secular 64
Fugitive notes on certain cantatas and motets of J S Bach 64
Widor, C M 57, 95
Wilcken, A M *see* Bach, Anna Magdalena 26

Wilhelm Ernst, Duke, of
    Sachsen-Weimar 19, 20
Williams, C à B 97
Williams, G 96
Williams, P *Bach organ music*
    68
Wilson, Sir S 91
Winschermann, H 105
Wise virgins 79
Das wohltemperiertes Clavier
    24, 47

Wolff, C 77, 106
Wolff, S D 105
Wolffheim, W 91
Wood, Sir H 97, 104
Wright, D 97
Wüllner, F 94

Young, P *The Bachs, 1500-1850* 60

Zadora, M 96
Zimmermann's coffee house 32